THE
CAGED
PANTHER

THE CAGED PANTHER;

Ezra Pound at Saint Elizabeths

by Harry M. Meacham

"But in the caged panther's eyes:

'Nothing. Nothing that you can do . . .' "
(Pisan Cantos, LXXXIII)

||||

Twayne Publishers, Inc.
New York

For Lucy

Preface

No MAN has precisely the same relationship with two people, not even with members of his own family, and so it follows that Ezra Pound's letters to me are unlike his letters to anyone else. I believe that in the perspective of history, every event, every word that touches the life of one of the great literary figures of our time is important, so I decided to publish this correspondence. What he wrote about his relations with *Poetry* magazine and Harriet Monroe, and how and why he broadcast over the Rome Radio, will be helpful to literary historians when the definitive account of these events is written.

This was the simple task I set for myself: to publish some letters with annotations. Since these communications turned on Pound's imprisonment and on efforts to free him, it was inevitable that in trying to learn what was at the other end of the string, I should find, first my interest, then my sympathies, captured by the lonely figure of this genius en route to his own special hell. As I pulled and probed, I opened a veritable Pandora's box of human frailties: ambition, greed, pride, cruelty, fear, and arrogance. I also found compassion, selfless devotion, and hope. And I discovered so many careless errors and deliberate distortions that the scope of my book was enlarged.

Robert Frost's mythic account, or accounts, of events leading up to Pound's release as well as the conflicting stories that appeared in news media have resulted in so much confusion that it is impossible to ascertain from hitherto published books about Pound just who did what, and when. For example, Pound's own lawyers, in writing about the case, jumped to

7

the wrong conclusions once they got away from direct testimony and legal technicalities.

In the light of all this, and because recollection of the events
will dim with each passing year, I decided it would be worth
while to go back to the record, to the events themselves, and
to the principals, including the protagonist, while memory
still holds. This is my report.

Students of Pound will see at once that I have broken some
new ground, but I hasten to add that this is due more to luck
than to scholarship. I had the good fortune to enjoy a special
relationship with Pound himself, based more on personal, than
literary grounds, and I have enjoyed the friendship and the
confidence of Dorothy Pound since 1957. She has clarified
many doubtful points and, most important of all, she has given
me permission, as the Committee for Ezra Pound, to publish
his letters. That great lady deserves a book of her own, and
I hope to live long enough to write it.

But my good fortune did not stop there. Professor G. Giovannini, of The Catholic University of America, in Washington, has opened his confidential files to me, and we have talked
for days on end about his conversations with Dorothy and
Ezra Pound. If that were all my debt could never be paid,
but beyond that, he has read this manuscript and made many
valuable suggestions. This is not to say that he approved of
the way I treated some of the poet's peccadilloes, but I did
have the advantage of his scholarship, his judgment, and the
enormous amount of information he had accumulated on the
Pound case.

There is no need to summarize the activities of Archibald
MacLeish, for they are set forth in detail in the body of this
account. It was not difficult to describe his role, for he was
consistent through all the years of Pound's incarceration. The
difficulty arose in persuading him to make his records available.
His modesty and his generosity permitted the Frost myth to
find its way into every book about the poet written since

April 1958. In 1960 I asked him to set the record straight, and many times after that by letter and in person, I tried to persuade him to write about the events or permit me to do so. He always replied courteously, but firmly, that he did not care to comment publicly on his role.

Finally, in going over my notes in September 1966, I again stumbled over the gap only MacLeish could fill, so I wrote to him again. On September 8 he answered from the Carlyle Hotel in New York: "I think we *should* talk," but he was leaving for Yugoslavia for three weeks and suggested that I call him at his home upon his return. "I agree," he continued, "that the time has come to settle the myth—if it ever can be settled." And he added the most important postscript I can find among my letters: "Why don't you look at the Frost, Eliot, and other letters to me on this subject in the L[ibrary] of C[ongress]?" And so it was that the gap was filled and the story of Pound's release was rounded out. I should add that we have not discussed this file since I spent several days going through it, although I did ask for, and promptly got, his help in procuring a copy of the letter he drafted to the Attorney General, which was signed by Eliot, Frost, and Hemingway. I am sure future literary historians will echo my expressions of gratitude to Archibald MacLeish.

While other acknowledgments will be found in the appendices I should like to record a special note of thanks to Mrs. T. S. Eliot for permission to quote from certain unpublished letters her husband wrote Archibald MacLeish. I am also grateful for permission to include some of Eliot's published writings. I am grateful to Bo Hammarskjöld for permission to print the letters of his late brother, Dag Hammarskjöld. I wish to thank Professor Lewis Leary, Witter Bynner, Mrs. Van Wyck Brooks, Mrs. Winfred Overholser, Donald Hall, George Dillon, and William Benton for permission to use their letters and other material. I am especially grateful to James J. Kilpatrick for permission to quote his editorial, which

appeared in the *Richmond News-Leader,* as well as his article
in the *National Review.* I am also deeply indebted to Mrs.
Ernest Hemingway for permission to paraphrase her husband's
letter to me, as well as excerpts from several of his letters to
Archibald MacLeish. I also wish to thank Donald E. Thompson and R. E. Banta for information about Pound's departure
from Wabash College.

I want to thank Hugh Kenner for his help and encouragement. He was the first person outside the family circle to read
the early draft of this book. He made many helpful suggestions then, and I have called upon his vast store of Poundiana
many times since his return to California. Giacomo Oreglia,
lecturer in literature at the Italian Institute in Stockholm, has
graciously permitted me to publish his interview with Pound.
Most of all, I am grateful to Ezra and Dorothy Pound for
their friendship and their confidence. My thanks are also due
to the companies and the people who made this book possible,
especially Frank Kirk. However, any errors in, or omission
from, the acknowledgments here and in the appendices, are
my responsibility.

Richmond, Virginia   HARRY M. MEACHAM
May 30, 1967

Contents

PART ONE

EZRA POUND, who is at the center of modern literary history, was born in the frontier town of Hailey, Idaho, on October 30, 1885, of New England forebears. He was the son of Homer L. and Isabel Weston Pound. His paternal grandfather, Thaddeus Coleman Pound, was a member of Congress from Wisconsin, and his mother was a great niece of Henry Wadsworth Longfellow. His father was Registrar of the United States Land Office at Hailey, but a few months after Ezra's birth he became an assayer at the Philadelphia mint, and the family moved to the suburb of Wyncote, Pennsylvania.

When Pound entered the University of Pennsylvania in 1901 at the age of fifteen, he formed two lifelong friendships, one with a fellow student, William Carlos Williams who would also become a major poet, and the other with Hilda Doolittle (H. D.) who was attending nearby Bryn Mawr. She became one of the best of the Imagist poets. In 1903, angry with the professors and disgusted with the curriculum, both to become chronic irritations, Pound withdrew from the University and entered Hamilton College, which granted him a Ph.B. in 1905.

Several reasons for Pound's withdrawal from the University of Pennsylvania have been advanced. Some biographers say his father was dissatisfied with his grades; others attribute his decision to a dispute with some of his teachers. His reasons went much deeper. In "How I Began," an article that appeared in T. P.'s Weekly[1] (London) June 6, 1913, he says he knew what he wanted to do at the age of fifteen. He resolved to know more about poetry than any man living. "In this search," he wrote, "I learned more or less of nine foreign languages. I fought every university regulation and every professor who tried to make me learn anything except this, or who bothered me with 'requirements for degrees'."

In spite of his disenchantment, he returned to the university as a Fellow in Romance Languages and Literature, and became an instructor while earning his M. A. degree. Pound then spent a year traveling in Spain, Italy, and France, as a Harrison Fellow in Romanics, and when the fellowship was not renewed in 1907, he accepted a teaching offer from Wabash College, Crawfordsville, Indiana. On one bitter cold evening the poet went out to mail a letter, and he encountered a girl from a stranded burlesque troupe. Since she was without friends or money Pound took her home, gave her his bed, and slept on the floor. The next morning he left for an early class, and she was discovered by his landladies, the Misses Hall, who immediately reported the incident to the college authorities. Conflicting reports obscure the details of the poet's sudden departure. Pound says he was dismissed as being too much the Latin Quarter type. Wabash records suggest that he resigned under pressure.[2]

As it turned out, this was to be the story of Pound's life. He would not be a mere spectator; he would become involved in mankind, and this involvement would eventually lead to the Rome Radio, the "gorilla cage" at the Disciplinary Training Center at Pisa, and to St. Elizabeths Hospital. Pound's commitment to life would also result in the publication of T. S. Eliot's poem "The Love Song of J. Alfred Prufrock," and James Joyce's *Ulysses*, and in the recognition in America, of the poetry of Robert Frost.

Pound returned from Indiana to the family home at Wyncote and urged his father to finance another trip to Europe for further study. The elder Pound agreed, provided Ezra could get a favorable opinion of his poetry from an "expert." Ezra showed some of his poems to Witter Bynner, one of the editors of *McClure's Magazine*. Bynner not only praised the poetry highly, but later persuaded Small, Maynard and Company to publish the first American edition of Pound's verse.

In January, 1908, Pound landed in Italy, remaining just long enough to publish in Venice, at his own expense, one hundred copies of his first collection of poems, *A Lume Spento,* before setting out for London. Describing his arrival on the London literary scene, his friend Wyndham Lewis wrote, "He was a drop of oil in a glass of water." The British "were unready to have their shortcomings as to literary taste dissected, to have their chronic amateurism exposed." In commenting on Pound's services to letters during the London years, including his success in having Lewis' novel, *Tarr,* serialized, he wrote of Pound's "critical sympathy; in every fact a creative sympathy."

In 1909 Elkin Mathews, of London, who had brought out William Butler Yeats's *Wind Among the Reeds,* issued *Personae,* Pound's first commercially published book (he later adopted the title for his collected poems). During the twelve London years Pound published a dozen books including his own poetry, renderings of the Provençal poets, and translations of Anglo-Saxon, Latin, and Japanese poetry. He also gave encouragement and aid to unknown poets that crossed his path. He was the moving force behind the revolutionary movements as Imagism and Vorticism.[3] In writing of the first anthology of the Imagist group, *Les Imagistes,* Pound said, "I was able to start a process to desuetize (i.e., take the cold fat out of) current poetry." When Amy Lowell came to London and took over the movement, Pound changed its name to "Amygism" and moved on to Vorticism with Wyndham Lewis and Gaudier-Brzeska, the sculptor who did the magnificent hieratic head of Pound that now stands in the garden of his daughter's castle at Merano, looking up the Adige Valley.

As he was running low on money, Pound obtained a job lecturing on medieval poets at the Polytechnic Institute in London. During these busy years he also found time to become foreign editor of *Poetry.* He used the magazine to advance the work of such poets as Rabindranath Tagore, Richard Aldington, T. S. Eliot, and a host of others, including Robert

Frost. He accompanied the New England poet to his publishers, snatched the first copy of Frost's first commercially published collection, *A Boy's Will*, and wrote a glowing review for Harriet Monroe's new poetry journal. In preparing her for the notice, he wrote her associate Alice Henderson, "Have just discovered another Amur'kn Robert Frost. Vurry Amur'kn, with, I think, the seeds of grace. . . ."[4] In 1920, Pound moved to Paris.

During the 1920's Paris was the artistic center of the world. Pound, James Joyce, Gertrude Stein, Pablo Picasso, and other writers and painters created an intellectual and artistic vortex that drew young writers from the rest of the continent as well as from England and the United States. In *Guide to Kulchur*, Pound wrote, "From 1830 to 1917 France was European civilization." The Paris years were productive ones, for he published "Hugh Selwyn Mauberley," considered by many critics to be his best poem, as well as *Umbra* and *Instigations*. He also edited T. S. Eliot's *The Waste Land*, and with $75 advanced by his wife Dorothy, he largely financed Eliot's book, *Prufrock and Other Observations*. When I inquired about this money Mrs. Pound wrote, "This was later returned to me."

Paris lost its attraction for Pound in 1924, so he and Dorothy moved to Rapallo on the Italian Riviera. "If Paris had been as interesting as Italy in 1924, I would have stayed in Paris," he told D. G. Bridson, for a B.B.C. broadcast in 1959. "The life of the mind doesn't stay in one department fixedly." While many of his important works, both prose and poetry, as well as his opera, *The Testament of François Villon*, were written in Italy, he devoted most of his time to his "tale of the tribe," the *Cantos*.

In his introduction to *The Economic Nature of the United States*, Pound says, "For forty years I have schooled myself, not to write the economic history of the United States, but to write an epic poem which begins 'in the dark forest' crosses the purgatory of human error and ends in light, 'frai i maestri di che sanno,' among the masters of those who know.[5] For this reason I had to understand the nature of error." While Pound's interest in monetary economics and history was aroused about 1912, when he read Silvio Gesell, German merchant and economist (1862-1930), it was not until his "schooling" led him to Major C. H. Douglas and his Social Credit Plan that he became deeply interested in usury (Usura in the *Cantos*). He decided then that the nature of error was to be found in our economic system and the faulty teaching of history. He was convinced that history without economics is not history ("there is no use trying to understand history as a mere haphazard list of events arranged chronologically"), and he also saw the relationship of history, economics, and literature.

From around 1917 on, his economic thinking found its way into his epic, the *Cantos*, as well as his prose writings, and more and more he drew on the works of three American historians: Thomas Hart Benton, Alexander Del Mar, Brooks Adams, and the Chinese writings of Kuan Chung. When Pound visited the United States in 1939 to accept an honorary Doctor of Letters from Hamilton College, his extra-literary preoccupations shocked many of his friends, and his violent attacks on President Roosevelt, who, he said, was leading us into World War II, alienated some of his most devoted disciples.

Pound believed in the poet as seer, as the "antenna of the race"; but few believed his prophecies or accepted his views on economics, so he returned to Rapallo and in January 1941 became a regular broadcaster on the Rome Radio. Mrs. Pound wrote me in 1966, "Nothing is stronger than truth, except myth." No myth seems more firmly established than the canard that the poet broadcast for the Fascists, and many writers go a step further and label him a member of the Fascist party. In one of his letters to me from St. Elizabeths he wrote, "E. P. arrived at microphone with difficulty after nineteen years

effort against encroachment ON liberty." While a prisoner in
Italy he wrote his law firm in London, "A few essential facts.
I was not sending axis propaganda, but my own, the nucleus
of which was in Brooks Adams' works forty years ago and
in Kitson's published twenty-five years ago, and in my own
prewar publications. This was sent and stated to be sent at
least over the medium wave, on various occasions with the
preface, 'On principle of free expression of opinion on the
part of those entitled to have an opinion, Dr. Pound has been
granted the freedom of our microphone twice a week. He
will not be asked to say anything contrary to his conscience
or contrary to his duties as an American citizen.' These conditions were faithfully observed by the Rome Radio." The
record ought to be clear, also, on the allegation that Pound
was a member of the Fascist party. Professor G. Giovannini
quotes Camillo Pellizzi, at one time president of the Fascist
Institute of Culture, and a declaration signed by the Mayor of
Rapallo and some sixty citizens who knew the poet, that
Pound was not a member of any Fascist organizations.

Dr. Giovannini, who worked tirelessly for Pound's release
at close range (he was, and is, Professor of English at The
Catholic University of America, in Washington, D. C.) and
who visited him almost weekly for approximately six years,
wrote in The New Times, of Melbourne, Australia (he
couldn't get the article published in the United States): "The
mistake is made of considering the broadcasts and particularly
his denunciation of the Roosevelt administration, in isolation
from the large context of his work and career as a poet and
social-economic essayist." He goes on to say that the Pound
emerging from the broadcasts is the Pound who midway in
his career discovered economics and with it the full significance of Dante's infamous beast Geryon, and since then, he
has carried on a campaign of excoriation of the twin divinities,
usury and mammon.

This is not an apology for Pound's broadcasts, nor is it

an attempt to justify his peculiar form of anti-Semitism. His return to the Rome Radio after Pearl Harbor was a terrible mistake that has cast a shadow over his life and the lives of all who love him, but it was a mistake for which he has paid in full measure.[6]

Why did Pound seek the microphone in the first place? Not for money, for the few lira he received did not cover his expenses. Not to betray his country, for he spoke as an American citizen and for the Constitution. Had he renounced his citizenship he would not have been arrested, and had he broadcast in his own country and spoken out against the war and the administration, he might have remained a free man.

Pound broadcast because he was committed. In fact, the poet became involved in everything that touched him. As someone said, "wherever he was, it was the intellectual front line." He became involved in the future of Eliot, Joyce, Frost, Gaudier-Brzeska, and others because he felt they had something new to contribute. He was always the educator, and enjoyed talking to young people so he could drill holes in their heads and inject his own ideas of what constitutes an educated man. T. S. Eliot said Pound "has always had a passion to teach. In some ways I can think of no one he resembled more than Irving Babbitt."[7] But neither his instinct to teach, nor his strong animus against what he considered to be President Roosevelt's economic malpractices (he called it treason) could have drawn him to the microphone. He was motivated by the conviction that ideas are true only as they go into action. This is one of the dominant themes in the *Cantos* and in his prose writings, and those of us who knew Ezra Pound understood this.

While this could not have influenced the poet, for he had not discovered Sir Edward Coke at the time, it is interesting nonetheless to note that he found what he considered strong support for his broadcasts when he read Coke's *Institutes* and the article on misprision of treason: "In legal understanding it signifieth, when one knoweth of any treason or felony, and concealeth it, this is misprision, so called, because the knowledge of it is an ill knowledge to him. . . ."

Naïve? Wrongheaded? Beyond question. But he was not a traitor. Many have compared the case of Ezra Pound with that of Lord Haw Haw and Tokyo Rose, but this is a mistake, for the question of *intent* must be resolved. Pound's intent was to educate the American people.

The effect of the broadcasts was not what the poet or the Fascist government (for entirely different reasons) expected. Pound's good friend Riccardo M. Degli Uberti[8] said, "he seems to have been understood only by his enemies." They frequently involved matters so remote from the war that at one time the Fascists suspected him of betrayal and impounded his bank account as an enemy alien! In introducing a symposium of essays on Pound in the September 1946 issue of *Poetry* magazine, the then editor and Pulitzer Prize winning poet George Dillon wrote, "I confess that it is hard for me in my own mind, to disentangle Pound from the war. His voice is associated with a certain shack in the mid-African heat, and even more with a narrow, brilliantly lighted radio tunnel under Plymouth Harbor. There, in the invasion period, when we dialed the short-wave program, Pound was sometimes good for five minutes of modest entertainment. That is all it was, and I doubt whether any of us who listened to him felt anything but amusement, though we were not in a kindly mood. Pound, whenever we caught his performance, went on and on. But it was impossible to have any serious reaction." This was the response of an intellectual and a poet.

Shortly after Pound's arrest, T. S. Eliot wrote Archibald MacLeish asking what he could do in the way of enlisting poets and men of letters to ease Pound's situation and prepare for his defense. He said he had discussed the case with many people, including members of the armed forces, adding, "I have not heard a single voice express any desire except that

Pound should be let off as lightly as possible and that the whole affair might be forgotten as quickly as possible."

On July 26, 1943, a District of Columbia Grand Jury indicted Pound and seven other Americans who were broadcasting from Europe for treason. Only two of the eight were ever convicted. Indictments against three of them were dismissed for lack of evidence based on the decisions of the Supreme Court in the case *Cramer* v. *United States*, April 23, 1945. The court declared, "The crime of treason consists of two elements, both of which must be present in order to sustain a conviction: (1) adherence to the enemy, and (2) rendering him aid and comfort. . . . The acts must be intentional. *The intent sufficient to sustain a conviction must be an intent, not merely to commit the overt acts complained of but to betray the country by means of such acts.*" (Italics mine.)

Professor G. Giovannini has released his confidential papers on Pound to me so that together we may try to set the record straight. He has accumulated an enormous file on the case because he was close to, and part of, day-to-day events from 1946 on, but he made few notes of conversations with the poet because, as he said, he had no intention of writing anything about Pound except, perhaps, more studies on Pound and Dante. Fortunately, he did record a conversation with the poet about the *in absentia* indictment and his confinement near Pisa. Since the United States government records and countless articles I have read by investigators, attorneys, and reporters reveal one contradiction after another, Pound's own version ought to be on record.

In the account that follows I have paraphrased, but have not expanded, Giovannini's cryptic notes. I have included information from the hitherto sealed files of poet-statesman Archibald MacLeish as well as information I have gathered from correspondence and conversations with Mr. and Mrs. Pound and others close to events.

The poet told Giovannini the United States government never got in touch with him before or after Pearl Harbor to dissuade him from broadcasting. He added that he had never been formally notified by our government that an indictment had been issued against him *in absentia*: "I learned about it from *Time* or some other news source." He went on to say that "After news of the indictment had reached me I went to the American Embassy in Rome to protest that I was not propagandizing for the enemy. An attendant asked for my passport and disappeared. After half an hour I began to think I might be arrested and left."

The fog of war, the chaos, and the bloody events taking place just ahead of the Allied advance, have confused the actors in this Greek tragedy (as one of his friends said) so that it is impossible, with the information now available, to say precisely what Pound did when the Allies entered Rome, although a number of writers have tried to do so. The account of H. A. Seiber of the Legislative Reference Service of the Library of Congress, who made a report on the Pound case for Congressman Burdick[9] (and who had access to government files) differs from the chronology of two of Pound's biographers.[10] Three witnesses, Mrs. Pound, Pound's daughter Princess Mary de Rachewiltz, and a friend, Miss Olga Rudge, do not agree with each other, and their versions differ from those of Seiber and the biographers. It seems to me that Mrs. Pound, who was there, and who has lived with this tragedy for twenty-six years, should be able to recall the events with the greatest clarity. She has written to me two detailed letters about Pound's surrender and capture (both actually took place) three years apart, and they agree in essential details. In a letter from Rapallo, October 15, 1966, written in answer to some questions I raised, she repeats her recollections of the opening of the second act of this politico-legal and deeply personal tragedy:

E. P. was in Rome when it was taken and he walked out (in a pair of Degli Uberti's heavy boots, many years later restored to owner) along the only road going north not infested by troops —spent a night in the open and with some peasants—got to a junction where there was a train going North with a herd of the dismantled Italian army—finally arrived in the Tyrol, at the house of the peasants who had brought up Mary. Olga and I were in Rapallo; without news for many days. E. P. ultimately found his way back to Rapallo via various adventures along Lago di Garda and Milan—Two Japs in a restaurant, with a Confucius vol., etc., etc.

When the U. S. A. came through Rapallo, between Carrara and Milan, E. P. went to town to give himself up, as having lots of information about Italy which could be of use.

She goes on to say that neither the Americans nor the Italians understood him, and that he was sent away. Finally,

He was taken from Olga's house on the hill (where we were staying) by a couple of vicious Italian Communists[11] who arrived at the door when I was paying my weekly visit to old Mrs. Pound in town. They had guns so he made no struggle. They took him to the next village and Olga dashed after him. They were kept 3 or 4 days and interrogated continually. One Amprim was in charge. I came home about 6 p.m.—E. and O. both gone . . .

As a postscript she mentions her visits to the Disciplinary Training Center at Pisa. It was a shattering experience.

. . . and all the saga of my two trips to the camp, one in a strange car, the other in a camion with a New Zealand football team . . . with sandwiches, my first meat for weeks—and how I walked several miles to get home after seeing E. P., with an unknown doctor who took me to his home at Massa Carrara for the night —his antique house devastated by troops—his wife and son so kind—cold soup and hot milk was all the food they had . . . Why and how one survives! Poor E. P.

As ever
D. P.

In a touching tribute to her father on his eightieth birthday[12]

his daughter describes his arrival at Gais, where she grew up, "his feet all blisters." She goes on, "A few days after his arrival at my nurse's small farm came two S. O. D. (Südtiroler Ordungs Dienst) men with heavy rifles on their shoulders and all apparent intention of arresting anyone coming out of Italy . . . They allowed him to stay long enough for his feet to heal. Urged him strongly to go to Germany, gently hinting someone might be able to show him a pass over to Switzerland. But his Ithaca was Rapallo."

Giovannini has discovered in his files and sent to me, an account of yet another episode in this series of bizarre adventures never published in this country, so far as I know. A story by Damaso Riccioni that appeared in *Il Nazionale* September 4, 1955, with the caption "Con Ezra Pound Al Largo Di Salo'" reveals that the poet visited Serafino Mazzolini, Minister of Foreign Affairs of the Italian Republic at Salo' on Lake Garda, the capital of the remnants of the old government, after the collapse of Rome in 1944. It is logical to assume that Pound saw the minister while he was with his daughter in the village of Gais, which is in the lake country near Salo'. Riccioni reports that he found the poet in conversation with the minister at the latter's villa and that Pound talked about Imagism, the poetical patrimony of Greece and Italy, but particularly of Italy, Hitler, and Stalin. He reported that Pound defended himself against accusations over his "Anglo-Saxon radio transmission." In answer to the journalist's question about the duties of a citizen to put aside his own feelings, subordinate them, when his country was at war, Pound replied: "Socrates was accused of impiety and the subversion of the laws of his country; still he was not impious nor subversive, and subsequent history has shown this. I am accused of betraying my country, which I love as much as you love yours. But one, who like me, acts in the light of a truth interiorly felt, and foreseen, anticipates in the present a most certain future reality."

"Poets are somewhat like seers," Pound continued, "The value and the character of an action are judged from the point of view of repercussions in the boundless dimensions of time; that is to say, in the foreshadowing of what sooner or later becomes history. And history—and Schopenhauer also says this—often changes tomorrow the titles of chapters which today have a contrary sense. Today my countrymen (I wish they could read my pamphlet of two years ago, *Visiting Card*, for the explanation of some absurd aspects of this war) give to the present tragic chapter a title that they themselves will change tomorrow by compulsion of events resulting from the fatal game of ideals and interests in evolution.

Over the radio I tried to make my countrymen understand that my ideas are above warring factions, because they are inspired by a vision far above the relations among peoples. As a citizen I do not speak nor stand against my country; as a thoughtful man I stand for points of view which I consider closest to the aspirations of my free spirit, under the spell of a vision of a 'sacred union' of all the peoples called by destiny to lead humanity by virtue of their advanced evolutionary state, intellectual and social. Besides, my very own countrymen at a time not far hence will have to admit the correctness of my convictions, even if before that time they will have sent me to the electric chair . . ."

At the end of the interview Riccioni got into Pound's hired boat and as they were rowed to Salo' in the light of a splendid sunset, the poet seated himself next to the boatman, took one oar, and in rhythm with his strokes recited *sotto voce*, some English verse, which Riccioni reports Pound said were Milton's.

There are certain inaccuracies in this account; that Pound taught at "Harward" (*sic*) and was dismissed for subversive thinking is one example, yet the interview with Riccioni did take place, and Pound must have said some of the things

reported. As to the Milton reference, when one remembers
that Pound called Milton's god "a fussy old man with a
hobby" one suspects he was burlesquing the great English
poet.

To return to Pound's capture (or surrender), as the poet
was descending the hill from Miss Rudge's home at Sant'
Ambrogio to Rapallo under guard, he passed the eucalyptus
tree he had so often admired and picked up a seed, or pip
from the ground; he kept it with him during the months at
Pisa and the years at St. Elizabeths and, no doubt, still has
it. He mentions it several times in the *Pisan Cantos*:[13] "and
the eucalyptus bobble is missing" (LXXX) and "the cat-faced
eucalyptus nib/ is where you cannot get at it," and, finally, in
the same canto:

> So that leaving America I brought with me $80
>   and leaving England a letter of Thomas Hardy's
>   and Italy one eucalyptus pip
> from the salita that goes up from Rapallo . . .

When Hugh Kenner visited the poet at Sant' Ambrogio
in March 1965 he made some magnificent photographs of
Pound, and he gathered three seeds from this famous tree,
one for himself, one for Guy Davenport, and one for me.
Mrs. Pound has since enlarged the club by sending a pip to
Prince Boris de Rachewiltz, the poet's son-in-law, and a leaf
to Professor Giovannini.

Whatever history decides was the proper sequence of
events, it is a fact that the poet was arrested on May 5,
1944 and, after questioning, was transported to the Disciplinary Training Center in chains. Since an important section
of the *Cantos* was written at Pisa, the compound will come
to occupy an increasingly important place in literary history,
just as it will serve as an enduring example of man's inhu-
manity to man. It should be understood that it was not a
training center at all, for it housed the dregs of the United

States Army—killers, deserters, thieves, black marketers, and other criminals—many of whom were shot trying to escape, some before Pound's eyes.

The poet has referred to the place in conversation, although not often, and it is mentioned frequently in the *Pisan Cantos*, but a detailed description of the center came out of a conversation with Giovannini. He frequently referred to Amprim, an officer who came down from Genoa to question him. He identified and signed transcripts of his broadcasts over the Rome Radio (although he said later he was not permitted to read them), and he also identified the typewriter on which they were written. He says he made it clear he had no intention of denying he was the author. Pound said the officer seemed surprised, "for he thought he had caught a traitor with thousands of dollars."

As Giovannini described the conversation, Pound drew a diagram of the Center with the medical area and drill grounds on one side, and on the other the maximum security area reserved for incorrigibles, trigger-happy black marketers, and the Lane Gang mentioned in the *Cantos*. At first, he was confined in this area in one of the ordinary cages. He then drew one line of cages, in back of which was a line of death cells, which no prisoner, he said, could endure for more than two weeks. He said the cells, apparently built of concrete, were for notorious malefactors and had an opening at the top "where sometimes one might see the hands of the prisoner poking out." Dust blown from a nearby road added to the acute discomfort of those incarcerated.

The poet did not remember how long he was kept in the ordinary cage, but referred to his stay in that section as "two months." Then he had what he called a breakdown and was transferred to the medical area. He said he was placed in the cage with the gruff order that no one was to talk to him and he was told that he might be there "for two days or two months."

Pound said the officers were afraid he might commit suicide or that the Fascists would try to rescue him (although he told one guard, pointing to fifty protruding spikes round about, that he could have easily slashed his wrists), so a special cage was constructed from heavy metal airfield stripping. For thirty-six hours during construction he had no rest, owing to the intense light of the acetylene torches. He described the dimensions of the cage as "about 6 x 6½ feet," and so when the army cot was given to him later, it together with the slops-pail left little room. At the beginning of his confinement in the "Gorilla cage" referred to in the *Pisan Cantos*, he had no cot, but he had been given six blankets, and so he slept on the floor. There was no roof. One morning after a heavy rain someone came around to see how he had survived and an army cot was ordered. At night a bright light, "a reflector," was trained on the cage; he could avoid the light only by covering his head with a blanket. Later he was given a pup tent when it rained.

The poet told Giovannini, "What saved me was my good physical condition. I had been playing from five to seven sets of tennis a day before my confinement." Later, it was decided that he needed exercise, and "subalterns" were appointed to accompany him. Pound says he directed one of them to a place behind a shack where he could sit while the guard marched up and down, and he instructed him how to manage the Italian language.

Giovannini says the poet told the story in a subdued voice, without visible emotion and without one word of complaint. Most of his account was in the third person, as if the memory of the caged creature were that of another, unknown to him. "When at one point I showed emotion at this treatment of him," his friend continued, he said "others had suffered more than he."

But in the caged panther's eyes:

"Nothing. Nothing that you can do . . ."[14]

The incommunicado was broken by rare visits. Mrs. Pound (who for a long time did not know where he was confined) was allowed two visits, and his daughter, Mary, also visited him.

There is little to smile about in the account of those terrible months, but Pound did recall one amusing incident. One of the guards instructed him to salute when an officer passed, but a lieutenant protested that "this was not according to regulations since I was a civilian, but I said I didn't mind. I had nothing to do."

On November 17, 1945 Pound was flown to the United States and lodged in the District of Columbia jail, and on November 26, a superseding indictment for Treason was returned against him. Ten days later he stood mute on arraignment, and a plea of "not guilty" was entered by the court. On December 4 he was taken to Gallinger Hospital; and on December 14, following their appointment by the court, four psychiatrists said it was their unanimous opinion that the poet was suffering from a paranoid state that rendered him unfit to advise with his counsel or to participate intelligently in his case.

On January 18, 1946 the court granted a motion for a formal statutory inquisition to determine the poet's sanity. The same psychiatrists declared him incompetent to stand trial, and in three minutes the jury found him of unsound mind and he was placed in the criminal lunatic ward of St. Elizabeths in Washington, D. C. In 1947, following an unsuccessful motion for bail and protests against his confinement among the spoon-and-gown inmates, he was moved to Chestnut Ward.

In answering the question "Recreation?" for his sketch in the British *Who's Who*, Pound wrote, "The public taste."

For fifty years my recreation has been poetry, and now, following my retirement, my recreation has come to dominate my life. Since 1912 or thereabouts it has not been possible to read poetry seriously without encountering Pound and his influence. Although I make no claims to Pound scholarship, I have known and enjoyed his poetry for half a century. Finally, through his published letters and the literature growing up around his work, I came to know this great poet and to admire him—not for his philosophy of economics, which I have never understood, nor for his racial and political pronouncements, but because of his character, his strength; because he was sincerely against so many accepted but questionable aspects of modern life; and because he was that rarest of creatures—a man of letters who was also a man of action. As I grew to know him personally, I learned that his political and racial views were not at all what I had thought they were. In short, I became deeply attached to him.

During the early years of his confinement at St. Elizabeths I thought very little about Pound the individual, but when I did think of him it was with a feeling of guilt. Like millions of literate Americans, I was content to listen to his nightingales while ignoring the old man rotting away in a filthy madhouse. Where many influences are at work, as in the Pound case, it is difficult to say precisely what galvanizes one into action. I think I was finally drawn into the fight by the activities and the writings of Archibald MacLeish.

In writing about the draft of eleven cantos called *Section: Rock Drill* in the *New York Times* of November 16, 1956, Mr. MacLeish closed his critique with this eloquent passage: "Not everyone has seen Pound in the long, dim corridor inhabited by the ghosts of men who cannot be still, or who can be still too long. . . . When a conscious mind capable of the most complete human awareness is incarcerated among minds which are not conscious and cannot be aware, the enforced association produces a horror which is not relieved either by the intelligence of doctors or by the tact of administrators or even by the patience and kindliness of the man who suffers it. You carry the horror away with you like the smell of the ward in your clothes, and whenever afterward you think of Pound or read his lines a stale sorrow afflicts you."

This article, and pleas by Hemingway and others, finally got me involved. These, and the knowledge that Tokyo Rose and other convicted traitors had been freed while our greatest poetic intelligence, never convicted of any crime, was being held, and seemed likely to be held until his death, as a political prisoner in a country that prides itself on political freedom. If I had any reservations they were swept away by the nobility of his bearing.

I was to find a ragtag bunch of camp followers making a great deal of noise and actually obstructing serious action by distinguished scholars like Professor G. Giovannini of The Catholic University of America and Professor Craig La Drière, then at the same university, but since 1965 at Harvard. Their noble exertions have all but been forgotten, just as their voices were almost drowned by the shouts of the rabble.

In command by virtue of position, achievements, and entree, not only into all news media, but into the highest positions in the government, I found the powerful battery of MacLeish, Hemingway, Eliot, and Hammarskjöld. The friend who refused to quit (Frost's statement to the contrary notwithstanding) was Archibald MacLeish. He was the first man Pound asked to see when he was confined at Pisa, and, when the time was ripe, he brought about the shifting of the iceberg, Robert Frost.

A full-length biography—or a dozen, for that matter—would not reveal the many facets of this Protean genius. Since this book focuses on Pound's years at St. Elizabeths—how he got there and how he got out—I am afraid his figure will be blurred unless I call on two excellent reporters to highlight the picture: Giacomo Oreglia and the poet himself.

I believe the following interview, which appeared in the liberal Stockholm newspaper *Dagens Nyheter* on November 5, 1958, over the byline of Giacomo Oreglia, and Pound's comments on the story, will help make the poet intelligible, and will set the stage for the letters that follow. The interview is an important literary document because it prompted Pound's comments on events and dates. This is just one instance in which he attempts to set the record straight.

The reference to Eliot's "having left out many important things in the collection of essays he has put together" probably refers, according to Hugh Kenner, to Eliot's having declined to include Pound's essay, "Mang Tsze: The Ethics of Mencius," which appeared in *The Criterion*, a London quarterly edited by Eliot. Pound is also quoted as having said that Kenner cut some of the essays "in a very rude way" in his excellent book, *Gnomon*. Mr. Kenner told me he did not cut anything.

Giacomo Oreglia: *Meeting Ezra Pound*.   (Sort of a translation)
Dagens Nyheter, Stockholm, Sweden. November 5, 1958.

Showing old-fashioned chivalry Ezra Pound, together with his wife Dorothy Shakespear, a finely built, reserved lady, and his amiable, well-educated daughter Mary de Rachewiltz met me at some distance from Castel de Fontana.

In the 13:th cent. Castel Fontana was built on old Roman ground. Shortly after the Second World War Boris de Rachewiltz bought it. Of all the old castles in Sud-Tyrol none is more wrapped in old tales. People are whispering of great riches buried in the ground and known only to the devil. I was also told, by the local inhabitants, that one, at night, can see burning fires on the battlements and a gigantic, golden calf close to the castle. Those legends don't frighten Ezra Pound. He is a sporty and agile man of medium height. His hair is silver white, his eyes steel grey, sometimes flashing with a piercing fire. When walking he sometimes favors a wooden cane, but in spite of his seventy-three years and the hardships he has met with, he seems far from tired and finished, and it's difficult not to be excited by his nervous vivacity and rapid changes of moods. He wears a dark shirt and linen trousers. There's nothing eccentric in his way of dressing. His wife and his daughter are also very simply dressed. A rapid glance might give you the impression of an everyday burgher-family out picnicking.

Pound seems pleased when I tell him I'm sent by a Swedish paper he knows well, and he immediately starts to talk about his Swedish acquaintances and friends. First of all Bo Setterlind—both E. P. and his wife talk beamingly about his B. S.'s visit in the U. S.—and Lars Forssell, with whom he has exchanged many a hearty letter. He also talks, with warm sympathy, about Dag Hammarskjöld—recently he has been reading his speech on Linnaeus, and he is very grateful for all H. has done for him, but, he suddenly says, in that imaginative and metaphor-rich language which is his own—"Many think I'm still a soul gone astray. I've spoken well of the secretary general of U. N., but I don't want to tie a tin can round his leg."

Pound speaks an Italian impressive by the amount of words he knows and the outstanding linguistic imagination. Sometimes he pauses, for a short while, and one who is not used to his way of talking may easily think he's lost the thread. But then, fast as an arrow, comes the absolutely perfect and precise word.

We go on talking about Swedish culture and E. P. says he has a lot to thank Swedenborg and Linnaeus for, the latter thanks to his strong and compact language—every word stands for one thing. A prose like that would be something for my grandson, Siegfried Walter, to practice on.

When Pound sees the collection of Forssell translations I've brought with me, he complains bitterly about being too old, otherwise he would have learnt Swedish, the most melodious language next to Italian, he thinks.[1] The pace of the dialogue goes up. E. P. shows himself to be a talker of high quality, much amused by intellectual word-fencing, by funny stories and sharp remarks. If a small witty thing amuses him, he'll burst out laughing loudly, or he'll wink maliciously or smile a little, but then, as soon as we touch on questions which really interest him, he'll become very serious.

When I directly hit upon one of the causes for my visit, my wish to control the amount of truth involved in some newspaper remarks E. P. is said to have made shortly after his return to Italy, he suddenly bursts out, saying: "All those guys (fellows,

people) have been writing a damn lot of lies, and, he says, laughing and very surely, "when journalists don't lie they're kicked
out of their jobs."

It doesn't take long to convince me that many Italian journalists have distorted or directly falsified Pound's own words.
Ardently E. P. tells me to be exact, now and then he grabs my
notebook from my hands and writes down some sentences he
considers to be very important, and at the same time he ironically
points out that I shouldn't think he suffers from [a] persecution
complex.

E. P. tells me about the different periods in his life, from the
day he left the U. S. in 1908 and printed his first poems in Venice,
at the age of twenty-three (ed. 100 copies); about his stay in
London from 1909 'til 1920 (the British used to call him, because
of his unconventional behavior, either "the singing cowboy" or
"the Idaho kid"; when he founded Imagism about his time in
Paris from 1920,[2] when he wrote a work which are among those
he himself likes the most, "Homage to Sext. Prop.," and about
his return to Italy in 1924, when he settled in Rapallo.

More than any other artist in our time E. P. has loved Italy.
Unluckily enough this love was connected with sympathies for
the fascist regime, which caused Pound to be accused, by the
Americans, of high treason.

During the war E. P. spoke from the Rome station of the
Italian radio and defended some of the propaganda-theses of the
axis-powers. But one has to keep in mind that he interpreted them
on the basis of ideas that he had nourished himself for a long time,
ideas about "usury," about the "usury" of capitalism which inevitably leads to war, ideas he also developed in essays in *Lavor
E Usura*, published during the war.

When the fascist regime left Rome in 1944, he left, without
help from either Germans or fascist VIP's, walked for many days,
slept in barnyards and finally managed, after many a hardship, to
reach Sud-Tyrol, where his daughter lived. As soon as the allied
forces reached the northern part of Italy, E. P. surrendered to the
first American soldiers he met and asked them to take him to the
district commander. He was then sent to Genoa. Pound himself
thought they would ship him to America and put him on trial.
Instead he was brought to a Disciplinary Training Center located
outside Pisa and there he wrote the cantos he later called the
Pisan Cantos.

In this camp there were German prisoners,[3] but mostly Italians from black shirt companies (Brigade nere and Decima Flottiglia MAS) and also a couple of Frenchmen belonging to the Deat and Doriot movements, and some Belgian rexists, nearly all of them held for wartime crimes. It soon was, however, an official secret that E. P. was more sternly treated than the other prisoners. He was locked in a steel cage with concrete floor but without roof, the so called "gorilla cage," constructed only with him in mind, in the daytime exposed to the burning sun, in the night flooded by strong spotlights. Much of what has been told about his days in camp is, however, free fabulations, E. P. is now eager to point out.

Pound doesn't shrink from his past, but he doesn't want to blow life into it again. What has happened to him is now a passed experience. He also thinks he has paid his share, "if history shows he is in the wrong," he has paid with the concentration camp, the prison, the term at the insane asylum. But he's very angry if somebody wants to tag him "fascist." He's never belonged to the party, and, talking about this, he asks for permission to write down the following in my notebook:

"Every man has the right to have his ideas examined one at a time." And he continues: "I don't hate America. I've always been a true patriot, I haven't made propaganda for America's enemies, but against the inner enemies."

He wants to point out that people often forget that he never —as Henry James and T.S. Eliot—has renounced American citizenship and that he never has told American soldiers to desert, and, he continues:

This talk about treason must come to an end, because by now the charges have been withdrawn, even by circles of high standing in the U. S. I've behaved in accordance with the American Constitution, where it is said that one shall oppose the government when it works for interests which are not those of the country.[4] Before and during the war Roosevelt was the real enemy of the U. S. The treason was carried out in the White House, in the head organizations of American finance, not in Rapallo."

His contempt of Churchill is clearly visible:

"This conservative reactionary, enemy of the working classes in every country, dazzled by Mussolini as long as he thought it was only the Italian worker he wanted to get rid of, a false fighter for freedom, with no universal ideals whatsoever, only a defender of the privileged classes and British colonialism, the man who stupidly let himself be taken in by Stalin."[5]

Pound refuses to make any statements concerning Italy and Europe today.

"I've been away from Europe much too long to be able to judge the situation. One needs at least ten years to be able to say anything about that, and I don't talk about things I don't know anything about."

Talking about the touchy political situation in Sud-Tyrol, where the German-speaking minority is extremely well organized and held together in one whole block, whereas the Italians, even though they rule the province, are split up in many parties, E. P. makes a short comment:

"It's clearly seen through the history of Italy that the Italians, being individualists of an extreme kind, are more likely to fight amongst themselves than against strangers. It's always been like that: 'whites' against 'blacks,' Guelfs against Ghibellines, black against red."

The talk with E. P. is drawing toward a close, and I ask him how he spends his day.

"I rest and I read, mostly historical works which are needed for my poetry, and just now I'm doing some proofreading on the Canto 98."

Talking about some anti-Semitic ideas, which I remind him he's being accused of having, E. P. gives reference to the book "Guide to Culture," written in 1938 and dedicated to his Jewish friend Zukofsky, where he, word by word, has written: "Racial prejudices are an absurdity, they are the weapons of either intellectually bankrupt people or sheer paragraph-riders."[6] He then categorically denies he had any knowledge, during the war, of any gas-chambers being operated by the Nazis, and says:

"My anti-Semitism? I didn't know anything of what was going on in Germany.[7] And when has there ever been anti-Semitism in Italy? The Italians are not, as are the nordics, afraid of the Jews. Isn't it said somewhere that for every Genovese you get seven Jews?"[8]

Pound wants to put forth a wish for tomorrow: "More honesty and less talk." And being on the question of talk, he asks me to cut short a bunch of "truths" which have been published in Italian and foreign newspapers:

That he, for example, should have in his possession secret documents concerning monetary transactions between Roosevelt and Morgenthau. "Those documents," he assures me, "have been given publicity by the American taxation department, and anybody can read them."

That he, during the war and in Radio Roma, had uttered the following as a direct call for rough action: "The only thing you can do with an Englishman is knock him cold." E. P. wants to point out that this phrase was used in a private letter, in 1938, to the English author and painter Wyndham Lewis, his own personal friend.

That he is said to have commented upon Eliot: "He is worthy of this toothless old hag (i.e., England) where he is now a citizen. His only fault is that he adjusts himself." E. P. is very sorry Eliot has left out many important things in the collection of essays he has put together; he also accuses the compiler of the latest essay-anthology, printed in the U. S., Hugh Kenner (Gnomon) for having cut, "in a very rude way," some of the essays.

That he has said about Hemingway: "Hem too has sold himself to the god of the dollar." On the contrary he is on very good terms with the author of "Farewell to Arms." This is also proved by the hearty and friendly correspondence which, during the last months, has been going on between the two authors. "For a long time people have been trying to create enmity between me and Hem."

That he doesn't like contemporary Italian literature, which he is said to have defined as "nothing but vomit." This is contradicted by the English translation he has made of Enrico Pea's "Moscardino" and by the esteem he shows authors like Tozzi, Marino Moretti, Valeri and others.

Verifax to all on list.

Hotel Grande Italia
RAPALLO
7/59

DEAR HM

My friends are the most chaRRming people, and the sweetest natures that gawd ever lett livv. AND they serve or cd/ serve to show why the white or caucasian or european and ang/sax races are getting shoved off the earth and enslaved by Ooozenstein, Weinberg and similar individuals of alien stock.

> i.e. they have NO sense what bloody ever of TIME
> coherence
> collusion
> collaboration.

Oreglia's article is ten times stronger than I had any idea of. It came out in Nov. and only the passage of a benevolent young swede now in June, 28th to be precise. (Nov. 5 in stockholm) enables me to read it in translation.

DIVERS specific items that could have been QUOTED by people not in position to assert 'em without suicidal intent, etc. Herewith the translation with a few corrections. Also a few notes on one paragraph containing various errors. I have no idea where Oreglia got the misinformaton in that pp/2, on p. 3.

The notes apply to numbers in red (which will verifax not red) now put in the text.

Notes. (1) slight misunderstanding, spanish is melodious. What I had been driving at was the capacity of the Swedish for taking over sonorities due to the anglo-saxon element in english. As in my debt to the Seafarer, and Bib. Ibbotson's hammering anglo-saxon into me.

(2) Paris chronology always a bit puzzling. 1906, with Dondo, 1911, 1912 with Walter Rummel.
Post war, Hotel du Pas de Calais; 70 bis r. Notre Dames des Champs.

While we are at it, Italy: 1898, 1902, 1908, stray visits, Rapallo 1924-45 or 46 or whenever it was.

Propertius written in London, before Mauberley.
(3). This puzzles me. I don't know where Oreglia heard it. D. T. C. Pisa, solely for american soldiers, guilty of anything from mild inebriety, and AWOL, to murder, high-jacking, or sending home $15,000 in one week, origin of same unaccounted for. One particular hillbilly had been very active.

(4). slight confusion on O's part, between Constitution, Jefferson, Coke on "Misprision" but pretty accurate reporting in view of technical nature of the subject.

(5). Called a liar to his face by Joe S/—at least in the words: I will believe the American. (i.e. Truman).

(6). frequently so stated by journalists. The dedication is to Zukofsky AND Bunting, a jew and a quaker; an INDIVIDUAL jew and an INDIVIDUAL quaker.

(7). S. F. Pinter's letter, re Father Gander, in recent issue of Our Sunday Visitor, shd/ be read by every recipient of this VFX.

(8). Local proverb is: it TAKES three jews to beat a genovese.

PART TWO

IN MAY 1957 I requested permission to visit Pound at St. Elizabeths. The die was cast.

(1)

S. LIZ.   27 Marzo

DEAR H. M.

You won't interfere with anyone, but I can't notify everyone else to stay away, so as to assure you uninterrupted etc.

Usually fewer people on Tu/ and Th/ BUT no use trying to calculate that. I take it you have no top secret, seditious subversive, moscovite etc. data to discuss.

Cordially yours

E. P.

If any emissaries of Satan barge in I will warn you of suspected evils.

On April 6, 1957 I climbed the stairs of Chestnut Ward, one of the oldest and most disreputable sections of the government mental institution in Washington, D. C. The poet strode forward to greet me and led me to an alcove somewhat removed from the blare of a dozen radios and the distracting nonconversation of his fellow inmates. Mrs. Pound was present as well as a young student unknown to me.

Throughout the afternoon patients would approach our corner and whisper to Pound. He spoke to them softly and turned them away, always without losing the thread of the conversation. I had brought along his translation of Sophocles' *Women of Trachis* for his signature, and this pleased him. "I'm glad you have that," he said.

I told the poet at once that I was not interested in his political or monetary theories, and confessed that I knew little about either one. This amused him, for I was to learn that while he respected erudition, he respected intellectual honesty even more. In one of his letters to me he says that "honesty is a form of intelligence." And so this first, and for me somewhat awkward, meeting was the beginning of a strange and wonderful friendship—a friendship unmarred by the slightest unpleasantness.

We talked of the difficulty of getting poetry published, and he said it had always been so. I asked him why so many poets had turned to pedagogy. Was this the result of what L. A. G. Strong called "the force of spiritual gravitation?" "No," he replied. "Generally a man is drawn to the teaching profession because he is associated with people inferior in learning.

"When I first went to England they were just catching up with Browning. I was considered a promising young poet until I published the first of the *Cantos* and then I was given up for lost." Why did he not write his autobiography? "No! No!" Well then, his literary autobiography? "It's all in the *Cantos*. I was offered a large sum of money for something like that but decided to translate more Chinese instead." Does it matter that the average cultivated reader does not understand the *Cantos*? And why the preoccupation with economics and money? A shrug. "A poet writes what he has to write. All the great poets—Homer, Shakespeare, Dante —made history a part of their poetry."

We talked of Eliot and his position as literary arbiter. "Eliot has had his day. My time will come. A poet ahead of his time is like a small rudder on a big ship. His effect is gradual." And then, on another subject: "But when you talk about the poet's failure to communicate. Well, this has always been an issue." In a letter to William Carlos Williams, written in 1908 from London, he says, "As for 'eyes of too ruthless public' Damn their eyes. No art ever grew by looking into the eyes of the public."

Once on a December afternoon, Pound was sitting in my car reading his mail (he could not leave the grounds, or, in fact, be out of sight of the ward). This was one of the two

high spots of the day, the other being, of course, the arrival
of Dorothy Pound and his visitors. Letters came from
students all over the world. As he read them he chuckled and
said, "They relate everything I've written to Browning." On
opening another letter he said, "This is from behind the Iron
Curtain. My friend says he has every book I've written hidden
in the secret compartment of a safe, and elsewhere."

Years before I had conceived a great admiration for Dr.
Oliver St. John Gogarty, Irish poet, patriot, wit, and surgeon.
And so, when I became president of The Poetry Society of
Virginia I invited him to Richmond for a reading, and we
entertained him in our home. He talked of the little people
and Yeats and of his friendship with young Joyce. He said
he considered *Ulysses* the greatest literary hoax in history.
And he impersonated Edith Sitwell: "The last time I saw
her," he said, "she was dressed as a bishop." He spoke none
too kindly of Eliot, "England's greatest poet ever to come
out of St. Louis."

In the early days of our friendship I wrote to him about
his relationship with Yeats. He replied, in part:

Yes, I saw Shelley plain and he stopped and spoke to me. Yeats
used to assure me that there was more poetry written now than
at any period in the world's history. He knew nothing about
China. Yet there is much want of discrimination in the world
just now; witness the awards to T. S. Eliot and to that pretender
Ezra Pound. James Stephens used to say in a poem of which I
remember only the last lines:

> He caused policemens' feet to beat
> In the verse of Ezra Pound.

All this was fresh in my mind so I brought the conversation
around to the Irish literary revival. Mrs. Pound (a great lady
who deserves a book of her own) said, "I knew Yeats before
Ezra." This reminded me that Yeats greatly admired her
mother, Olivia. It was always difficult to get Ezra to talk about
the past and his friends; especially his benefactions. However,

he was interested in this period and said, "Yeats and Wyndham Lewis were allergic to each other. I would see Yeats on Monday and praise Lewis, and he would rage. Then a few days later I would see Lewis and praise Yeats, with the same result. Yeats could never learn a foreign language. He never learned French.

"Colum promised to be a first-rate poet, but he stayed in Ireland too long. Joyce saw as I did, that the French were forty years ahead of the English. Joyce's *Ulysses* was the end of a period, not the beginning." I steered the conversation back to Gogarty, but it was apparent Pound thought little of him. "He was a man of great physical courage," he said, "and a good doctor." And that was that.

As the shadows lengthened I tried to draw him out on the Paris days by mentioning that I had just reviewed a new edition of Gertrude Stein's *Stanzas in Meditation*. I added that at the very least I considered her a serious artist. His only comment was, "Well, her own brother called her an idiot."

The part I played in the last phase of the campaign to free the poet was a simple one, and the story is soon told. I conceived and carried out a letter-writing drive aimed at the office of the Attorney General and members of Congress. Since I was holding a full-time job, and a demanding one, I knew that in order to be effective I would need a list of prominent people known to be favorably disposed to the cause of Pound's release. I discussed the possibility of such a list with the poet, and my request prompted the following letter.

(2)

23 Sept. 57

DEAR H. M.

I should think the people to contact would be Lt. Gen. P. A. del Valle,

Troy Hill, bx 240 rte 4, Elkridge, Md.
(Marines, led at Okinawa, etc.)

If I can't find a copy of his article in Task Force, you

    might express a desire to see it.

                         There was stray copy

somewhere in this chaos.

Immediate correspondence with

Chas. Guenther, 29 35 Russell Blvd, St. Louis, Mo.

                         as they are getting ready

for poetry day/exhibit.

Archibald MacLeish, Uphill Farm, Conway, Mass.

W. C. Williams, 9 Ridge Road, Rutherford. Has as you know
recently broadcast.

Louis Dudek, also broadcast in Canada

                        I may find a copy of that if you
                        want it.

1143 Sixth Avenue, Montreal, Canada.

Prof. G. Giovannini

    4543 S. Dakota Av. S. E. Washington, D. C.

One of the best documented at present.

recent contact. Louis Maverick (economist).

    2027 S. Bentley Av. Los Angeles.

Dag Hammarskjöld. United Nations.

General J. F. C. Fuller   W. Poundgate Manor

                      Crowborough, Sussex, England.

Admiral Sir Barry Domville, Robins Tree,

              Roehampton Vale, London S. W. 5, England.

N. H. Pearson, 233 H. G. S. Yale Station, New Haven, Conn.

Geo. Slavin, 31 East Mary Av. East Providence, R. I.

John Theobald 1390 Merritt Drive, El Cajon, Calif.

If you write to Hemingway, Finca Vigia, San Francisco di Paula,
Cuba, do say that you have been here and that D. P. and I were
both very indignant about the lie in "Tempo" the Italian weekly,

quoted in Mr. Luce's "Time" as if it were the Roman daily. But equally mendacious.

Admiral John Crommelin, Harrogate Springs, Wetumka, Ala.

D. Horton, Apt. 14. 1419 Clifton Street, Washington N. W.

Robt. Furniss, 315 34th Street. Virginia Beach, Va.

British Who's Who clearly states I was NOT sending axis propaganda, but arguing re/american policy.

etc.

and do write to me about any further points you want my opinion on.

Gratefully yours

E. P.

e. e. cummings, Silver Lake, N. H.

Marianne Moore, 260 Cumberland St. Brooklyn, N. Y.
Frank L. Wright, Taliesin, North, Spring Green, Wis.

(3)

24 Sep 57

DEAR H.M.

Wrote yesterday to you at 400 E. Main
hope that address still functions.

If Dave H [orton] comes today, hope he will see you @ Shoreham and that you can at least get Giovannini on the phone.
    You might add to yr list Marshall McLuhan, St. Michael's College, Toronto, Canada and Olivia Rossetti Agresti, 36 Via Ciro Menotti, Roma, Italy.
    She has done life of Lubin, founder of internat. Ist. of Agriculture,
    and recently a magnificent chapter on him. was interpreter at Versailles, and at 83 knows as much of europe as anyone,
    AND of the fascist regime, which she did not wholly approve but to which she does justice for constructivity.
    particular emphasis on vocational representation. you were against complaining of particular lies and slanders. Might note, British Who's Who/re/my having freedom of microphone. the

formula: freedom to express opinion ON THE PART OF THOSE QUALIFIED to have an opinion.

was a contribution to thought and to better definition of proper limits
   (in case of radio and TV, the proportion of liberty to time at disposal is important.)

E. P. arrived at microphone with difficulty / after 19 years of effort against encroachments ON liberty.

A frequent refrain was: This is what Brooks Adams published in 1903 (or in 1897).

CAN this be axis propaganda??

He always spoke as an american.

Though not engaged in espionage for the u.s. govt. it was his DUTY to learn as much as possible re/ what happened on the other side of the line /

                                                                which could have been useful

TO the U. S. after defeat of Italy.

a far-sighted foreign office would want to contact the HONEST men in the defeated country, not to take up with the double crossers who are just as ready to betray the U. S. as they were to double X anyone else.

On quite another line, it probably has not occured to you that I am not raging to get back to Italy,

   that I wrote a couple of cantos re. T. Jefferson before I did longer ones on Adams/

that I am INTERESTED in the U. Va, though never had any connection or pipe line thereto,

   That I wd/ be interested to carry on the job T. J. intended. i.e. he was interested in civilization.

And my wife's connections go back to that Tucker who married John Randolph's ma, and brought out a Blackstone before that family retired to Europe again.

Of course, I am not out of the bughouse yet. But this is probably an angle that hadn't occurred to you.

The States Right angle goes back to what was possibly the first course in Reconstruction History, given by H. V. Ames at the U. of Penn in 1901 or 02.

One doesn't have time to get around to all possible topics in two afternoons.

Yrs
E. P.

(4)

24th Sept. 1957 (later)

DEAR H. M.

Re/ one of yr/ questions. I don't see that it is anyone's damn business WHAT I wd/ do IF I got out.

It is unConfucian to make plans for circumstances that cannot be calculated.

It would depend on HOW I got out.

As I always spoke as an american, FOR the constitution, etc. it wd/ be a joke of jokes to get out ON CONDITION that I return to Italy.

I would naturally prefer to go live with my daughter to staying in the bughouse.

After all [Senator William E.] Borah did say: "Waaaal, I'm sure I don't know what a man like you would find to do here?"

God knows I can see PLENTY that needs doing. HERE.

And the present state of Italy is no picnic, the place has been largely ruined by two of the greatest shits mankind has known, Roosevelt and Churchill, and even Churchill wanted to attack thru the Balkans so as to save a little civilization,

AND that would have brought the russian savages into Europe.

etc.

cordially yours, I will add reflections as they occur to me.

EZRA POUND

In 1939 I had got my affairs into enough order so that I was planning to spend about two months of the year IN the U.S.

as one could have got into a taxi in Rapallo and gone on board at Genoa. and the Rex wd/ have brought one in 5 days to N. York.

EP

(5)

S. ELIZ   10 Oct 57

DEAR MEACHAM

I thoroughly agree with you that I should NOT be aware of what my friends are up to. Let each of 'em do his best for the general enlightenment but not have me puzzle out their per-dictaments. And I should extend the same principle to Dr. Over-holser who has several thousands of problems right here on the lot to be bothered about.

I shall be delighted to see you whenever you feel like a little conversation, and not merely when in search of service, whatever its magnitude.

The correlation of Poetry societies to text books is a service, considerations of which can't be disposed of in one or several afternoons.

cordially yours

EZRA POUND

(6)

S. ELIZ D.C.
14 OCT '57

DEAR MEACHAM

Nice note from Hem to D. P. stating he had not seen the lies in the press but only the quote in TIME to which he "paid no attention"

adding: "I could read each day that he denounced me and would no more believe it than I would believe that we did not live in Rue Notre Dame des Champs in the old days."

Which shows where the chief cormorant Luce has brought the credibility of his smear sheets.

Weakness in defense and research/ commentators on TV full of piety professed and professed patriotism

DARE not, or at any rate, do NOT mention

the chief cause of weakness.

Whether ANYone cd/ challenge them to do so, and get any results, you are in a better position to calculate than I am.

I don't think you shd/ have too narrow a program or bore people with my personal sorrows.

BUT with yr admirable aim to eliminate captivity of yrs. truly, you might mix a few germane ideas into yr/ conversation.

The DEGRADATION of text books. The failure of the professors to organize on FASCIST lines.

But don't use THAT word. Call

it professional organization/they have No organ in which to protest against abuses INSIDE their own profession/

no adequate mechanism to praise ADMIRABLE text books like Lind's recent Latin Poetry in English/ or even Preston's Chaucer.

No attempt is made to communicate with each other. No answer to my inquiry privately re/ men on their OWN faculties which gives name and address of intelligent members *of* the profession

No place to go into the behavior of the Foundations, or of the Harvard Press in particular.

No coherence in hammering on the abuse of professional time. If the poor fish are NEVER given time to cultivate their OWN minds, how the HELL are they going to energize the students and keep up with, say, Russian competition, not merely in space ships and means of transporting swine to the moon, with no intention of picking the worst swine and exporting them?

Somebody has got to tell 'em

And with McClellan and Mundt seriously asking (on TV) what they ought to do to clean up labor, somebody ought to say: do it in a manner homogenous with our OWN original system. Use our anglosaxon heritage. Division of powers/ legislative, executive, judicial INSIDE the unions, and secret ballot for or against Becks and Hoffas. who in their own eyes ANYhow, are no worse than advertised burucrats and politicians.

cordially yours

E. POUND

In our conversations and in my letters to Pound I had spelled out my "narrow" program to help get him out of the "bughouse." I wanted to go right down the line, avoiding all involvement in his extra-curricular activities. Many of his well-meaning friends had destroyed their usefulness by getting involved with the lunatic fringe. I had written Mrs. Pound: "The proposition is not justice, but freedom." I told Pound I thought there were two roads to freedom—he must capture men's minds or he must touch their hearts. I added that he was too far ahead of the pack to lead men down the first path, so we had no choice. And, after all, it was a bit late to talk about justice in the Pound case.

The September 9, 1957 issue of *Time* magazine carried excerpts from an interview with the poet published in Italy's conservative *Il Tempo*. In discussing contemporary authors he was quoted as having said, "In America, well, Papa Hemingway knows how to write, but he's dishonest." In a letter previously quoted Pound had asked me to write Hemingway about the "lie." I did so but held out little hope of a reply.

Some of the poet's Washington friends, as well as others interested in his release, had told me of writing Hemingway about the case and getting no reply, and some were critical of his failure to write to them or to identify himself with their efforts. The fact is that the great novelist worked effectively for Pound's release, but he went about it in his own way. When he hit, he hit hard. In the December 13, 1954 issue of *Time*, Hemingway is quoted as saying, "Ezra Pound is a great poet, and whatever he did he has been punished greatly and I believe should be freed to go and write poems in Italy where he is loved and understood. He was master of T. S. Eliot. Eliot is a winner of the Nobel Prize. I believe it might well have gone to Pound. There is a school of thought in America which, if encouraged far enough, could well believe that a man should be punished

for the simple error against conformity of being a poet.
Dante, by these standards, could well have spent his life in
St. Elizabeths Hospital for errors in judgment and of pride."
Hemingway's comment on Dante is interesting in this context, for that great poet was condemned to death as a traitor
to Florence and spent the last years of his life in exile. When
the novelist was accepting the Nobel Prize in Literature he
spoke out again in favor of Pound's freedom, and from the
world stage at Stockholm: "I would have been very happy
if the [Nobel] prize had been awarded to Mr. Pound."

Much to my surprise Hemingway answered my letter at
once. He said he had already written Mrs. Pound and told
her not to worry about such rubbish. He went on to say that
he had been in touch with serious people about Pound's release and felt things would be much easier but for some of
Ezra's friends, especially John Kasper. He said he never
answered their letters or dealt with them in any way. He
felt they were not interested in getting Pound out of St.
Elizabeths. They just wanted a cause.

Since Mrs. Pound's suggestions carried much weight with
Ezra, I turned to her with a most vexing problem, one that
troubled both MacLeish and Hemingway: Pound's intran-
sigence at a time when compromise seemed essential. We
were disturbed by newspaper reports about some of his
visitors and new-found friends. The papers made no distinction between the two, and the Pounds had no means of
screening those who wished to call, for whatever reasons,
although they could refuse to see them. All this added to our
difficulties when the tide was flowing in our direction, when
Mr. MacLeish was engaged in delicate negotiations and I
was soliciting letters to the Attorney General from prominent
people who were sympathetic.

As T. S. Eliot said,[1] "Pound was always a masterly judge
of poetry; a more fallible judge, I think, of men." And so,

unwilling to ascribe any but the highest motives to visitors, the poet continued to see those who called and to grant interviews to unfriendly writers who then tried to destroy him. Small wonder he disliked newspapermen.

In the light of all this I urged Mrs. Pound to attempt to persuade Ezra to sever relations with Kasper and a few others and to refuse to see reporters until the question of his freedom was resolved one way or the other. I concluded:

Perhaps it *is* asking too much, but if Mr. Pound should write MacLeish, Cummings, Dr. Williams or Eliot, pointing out (as he did to me) that he does not support Kasper, and, having learned of his activities, renounces him, and then suggesting that the letter be leaked to a friendly newspaper (if we could find one) much ground could be recovered. If he agrees I might be able to arrange for an interview along these lines.

I also wrote Ezra pointing out that Americans are basically fair, and adding, "A letter from you might light a fire. I seem to remember that when Sherwood Anderson wanted to quit work and devote his time to writing he composed a begging letter to a rich relative. He said later that a certain feeling came into his fingers. All he wanted was money." But nothing came of all this. In fact, it soon became evident that I had touched a raw nerve, for Pound returned again and again to his bad press.

(7)

Dear H. M.   23 Oct 57

Aren't you rather implying that there is a press that WANTS to print the truth or that will print a correction of any one partic-ular lie without simultaneously printing several new lies or slanted statements?

cordially yours

E. POUND.

Thanks for your kind letter.

(8)

29 Oct 57

DEAR H. M.

I have told Giovannini that I trust your sincerity. Have you
heard from MacLeish? And are you able to get ANY idea of what
he thinks about history, or whether he has ANY idea of my position
re/ balance of power in Europe or anything else?

Or whether he thinks you can collaborate with him?

Yrs

E. P.

The poet was well aware of what was going on "outside."
A few days after he had my letter to Dorothy he wrote
Archibald MacLeish, "The naïve but benevolent Meacham
beseeches a statement for the press. . . ." And again on
October 29, "Wot about Meacham? You heerd from him?
Va. Poetry Soc., mebbe nearer yr/ point of view."

In the following months I wrote to most of the people
on Pound's list. Some were eliminated because I felt that
their participation, however well-intentioned, might do more
harm than good. Dr. Giovannini also sent a long list, which
he had obtained from the Pounds and to which he had added
names. Some of the poet's friends wrote to me as well as the
Attorney General; a few of these letters are included in the
appendix. As an unexpected bonus, I formed many lasting
friendships as a result of this correspondence. The one I
cherish most is the bond I formed with the beloved poet
Witter ("Hal") Bynner. We corresponded until he was
totally paralyzed. On September 30, 1963 he wrote to Mrs.
Pound, "It has been through Ezra that Harry Meacham has
come latterly into my life."[2] While the poet was, for the
most part, ignored by press and public alike, every year or
two his name would appear in the news and there would be
a flurry of activity to get the charges against him dropped,
but these sporadic efforts were largely ineffectual. It is also

true that when his name appeared in print there were always a few strident voices to shout, "Shoot him!"[3]

Although the fact was unknown to the public and, indeed, to many of Pound's friends, there were at least four forces working independently (and sometimes at cross-purposes) exerting continuous pressure which would eventually bring the Pound case to the floor of the House of Representatives, to the personal attention of the Attorney General of the United States and, eventually, to the door of the White House. Governor Sherman Adams was brought into the case during the last few months of the poet's confinement.

It is not possible to mention the names of all who were involved at one time or another, briefly or otherwise, nor to separate all those who helped from all those who hindered. I cannot ignore, and neither can I evaluate, the activities of a small group of temporary Washington residents—artists, students, and the like—who frequently wrote letters to the newspapers. It is entirely possible that they were of some help, although their activities greatly disturbed Hemingway and others. But the three major identifiable forces were: (1) a group of scholars led by Dr. Giovannini, whose influence reached into academic circles in the United States as well as in England, Australia, and Italy; (2) Congressman Burdick of North Dakota, who on August 21, 1957 introduced House Resolution No. 403 calling for an investigation of the Pound case,[4] and a Senator (unidentified) who asked the Legislative Reference Service of the Library of Congress to make a study of the case (oddly enough, the Senator and the Congressman acted independently); and (3) the most powerful force, exerting pressure almost from the moment of Pound's incarceration, Archibald MacLeish. But I am getting ahead of my story.

I had written Mr. MacLeish about my visits with the Pounds, and I also told him what I planned to do. I said, also, that Mr. John Cook Wyllie, Librarian of the University of

Virginia, was most sympathetic, wanted to help, and had, in fact, written to the Attorney General expressing his concern that Pound was being held indefinitely, without trial. He was of the opinion, held by many, that the poet's best interests would be served if he were tried on the indictments for treason, since he felt a conviction would be impossible. In his reply Mr. MacLeish refers to the "principal obstacle," John Kasper.

ARCHIBALD MACLEISH   UPHILL FARM, CONWAY MASSACHUSETTS

Oct. 17 1957

DEAR MR. MEACHAM:

Thanks for your letter.

In my opinion there should be no public stir about the Pound matter at this time. Robert Frost and I have seen the Deputy Attorney General and we are satisfied that the Department of Justice is well aware that Pound cannot and should not be held longer. The problem is one of working out a disposition of the indictment (which should be nol prossed) arranging for Pound's future and finding the right moment. The principal obstacle now is Kasper.

You might tell Mr. Wyllie that the doctors are quite clear that Pound cannot stand trial—that the consequences of a trial would be disastrous regardless of the result and that Pound must not be subjected to it.

I have found Pound very reasonable and patient about the whole sad business and though I wish he would and could disassociate himself from Kasper I should never dream of suggesting to him that he do anything he doesn't want to do. It's his life and his sad fate and all the rest of us can do is to help as we can. Certainly it is for him to say where he should live within the limits of any conditions fixed by the Department of Justice.

In sum, I should say the best thing to do now is to inform the Department of Justice of one's interest and concern.

Needless to say, this letter is written in confidence and should not be quoted.

Again, my thanks.

A. MACLEISH

On February 24, 1958 I wrote to Senator Harry F. Byrd about the case. Identifying myself as one of his supporters I said, "I will be deeply grateful if you will have your secretary call the Attorney General and ask about the status of the Pound case." This seemed to me little more than a routine request, but I never heard from "that bird of a Senator," as Mr. MacLeish called him. And yet I didn't blame him. It was an unpopular, and to many must have seemed a hopeless, cause. Pound, lone actor in the literary tragedy of our times, had become a ghostly figure stalking the corridors of Chestnut Ward and occasionally haunting the conscience of the few who remembered him. In a statement serving as an addendum to his paper "The Strange Case of Ezra Pound" (*New Times*, Melbourne, August 26, 1955), Giovannini reported that, at a meeting of Modern Language Association at which the *Cantos* were being discussed, only one scholar knew of Pound's whereabouts, and then mistakenly assumed the poet was enjoying himself in a well-furnished apartment at St. Elizabeths and did not want to be released.

Early in my activities I recognized Kasper as a major roadblock and, as mentioned previously, I had (lacking Mr. MacLeish's reticence) warned the Pounds that he was a liability and should be charged off as a bad human investment. Hemingway and others who were involved or who thought of lending a hand, joined MacLeish in deploring Pound's association with the violent racist.

On January 30, 1957 the *New York Herald Tribune* carried the first of a three-part series on the Pound-Kasper relationship. The four-column front page spread was headlined "Segregationist Kasper is Ezra Pound Disciple," and it was accompanied by photographs of Pound and the racist as well as by a reproduction of a flyer issued by the White Citizens Council of the District of Columbia announcing a meeting at which "John Kasper, Segregation Chief, will speak." When

the story broke there was consternation behind the scenes.
I again urged Pound to renounce Kasper. He listened in
silence, and his only comment was, "Well, at least he's a man
of action and don't sit around looking at his navel." Giovannini, the kindest, most gentle soul I ever met, was shocked that
Pound's name should be linked with a man so intemperate
and inclined to violence and so he rushed out to the hospital
and talked to the poet for an hour about the relationship.

He spoke out against Kasper and how he discredited the
cause of conservatism. In reporting the conversation to me
the professor said he told Pound he thought it "melancholy,
miserable that at this time (when so much was being done for
his release) this obstacle should be placed in the way."

Pound listened attentively, for he loved and respected
him, but he was not disturbed by either the publicity or the
protests. He said, "If the whole of Europe had not fallen on
my head I might worry." He then talked again about his
trek north from Rome after the downfall of Mussolini, always
on the lookout for Partisans, witnessing atrocities, men lined
up against a wall near Rapallo and machine-gunned, adding
(to Giovannini's amazement, for this was the first he had
heard of it) that there was a reward of one-half million lira
on his head. He said he was not responsible for Kasper's
opinions. (He later wrote me, "I don't think you can show
any connection between my telling Kasper to read Confucius
and Agassiz and his present imprisonment.") Commenting
on the activities in his behalf by MacLeish, Hemingway,
Eliot, and at the last, Frost, he said that when the time came
"they" would release him, "Kasper or no Kasper."

Who was Kasper? This nobody who had a chance to be
somebody, but who ended his public career as a number in a
Federal penitentiary and a laborer in the workhouse in David-
son County, Nashville, Tennessee? Born in Camden, New
Jersey, in 1932, Kasper attended local schools, the Riverside
Military Academy in Gainsville, Georgia, Yanktown College

in South Dakota, and Columbia University in New York, where he earned a B. S. degree. Kasper had attended a poetry class at Columbia conducted by the poet and prosodist Babette Deutsch; this was his introduction to the poetry and criticism of Pound. He drifted to Greenwich Village, operated a bookstore for a short time, and moved in integrated social and literary circles in lower Manhattan and, from time to time, visited Pound at St. Elizabeths.

The poet wanted someone to publish American textbooks for students "who want first things first," and this resulted in the Square Dollar Series, published by David Horton and Kasper and boasting a blue-ribbon Advisory committee composed of Otto Allen of Notre Dame, Craig La Drière of The Catholic University of America, L. R. Lind of the University of Kansas, Herbert Marshall McLuhan of The University of Toronto, and Norman Holmes Pearson of Yale. While Kasper's connection with the series was brief, he was useful to Pound and did much of the research for *Gists from Agassiz*, which the distinguished scholar Guy Davenport called "an abominably printed but wholly admirable work." Kasper holds the copyright on this booklet. Kasper's usefulness soon ended, however, for he became chairman of the White Citizens Council in Washington and drifted south to Clinton, Tennessee where he was indicted for interfering with the integration of Anderson County High School. He was later found guilty of contempt for "violating a restraining order." He served two sentences in the federal prison at Tallahassee. His first conviction was for contempt of court and the second in connection with his activities at Clinton. He also served time in the workhouse in Davidson County, Nashville, Tennessee. He returned to Nashville and operated an automobile repair shop but was sued by the Volkswagen Company for infringing on its trademark. His Volkswagen Service Center was discontinued, and he became a salesman for a Nashville dealer in October, 1966.

In reporting to MacLeish I used the occasion to invite him to read at the annual meeting of The Poetry Society of Virginia at Phi Beta Kappa Hall, William and Mary College.

December 22, 1957

DEAR MR. MEACHAM:

I just don't know when I will get back from abroad and I don't dare say I'll be here in May. You are very good to ask me and I appreciate it more than I can say.

The Pound business looks cloudy from this angle. Robert Frost made a second trip to Washington and called on the Atty Gen whom (as Deputy Atty Gen) he and I had seen this summer. He came back reporting that he had a firm promise from Rogers to Nol Pros if St. Elizabeths would release Pound to a private sanitarium. Since that time nothing has happened and Mr. Frost's letters are not acknowledged. (Mine aren't either but I expect that from a Republican Administration.) I am going down next week and will see if I can gain entrance to the General. I think it most unlikely.

You don't suppose that bird of a senator of yrs could be interested in the case do you? His words are listened to by the Republicans—probably because the accent is similar.

Forgive my jibes. I am sick to death of the treatment we have been given over the past two years and I don't know how long I shall continue to sit on my typewriter—or the typewriters of all the others who want to burst out in shrill yells.

Faithfully

A. MACLEISH

I usually stayed pretty close to the main issue, but in one of my letters I listed some of the leading poets of the twentieth century, including, of course, Pound himself, William Butler Yeats, T. S. Eliot, and Robert Frost, and asked him to grade them. His answer is the only instance in which he showed the slightest impatience with my inanities. The truth is he never did enter into "purely tea party squabbles."

Perhaps I was naïve, but I couldn't get the idea out of my head that if an objective reporter or editor should quote

Pound on some of the great issues he had raised as well as the myths growing up around him, some good would come of it. I had friends who had friends on the *New York Times*, and my brother, William Shands Meacham, was Editor of the editorial page of the *Norfolk Virginian-Pilot*. Since my brother had introduced me to Pound's writings fifty years earlier, I had no doubts about his attitude toward the poet.

(9)

8 Nov, 1957

DEAR H. M.

Thanks again for your benevolence. Is the Norfolk [Virginian] Pilot a weekly or daily?

If you are talking to ANYONE who can get printed in the N. Y. Times it might be interesting to ask if ANY paper of large circulation ever objects to the lies in any OTHER paper of large circulation

when

said paper (say Mr. LUCE's TIME) refuses to correct a printed lie.

Rather interesting correspondence re/ Time's recent lie intended to make trouble between me and Hemingway. A line that has been used since 1939.

Hem is not taking the bait, but that does not diminish the shade or nuance of mendacity practiced in some quarters.

It is no time for me to enter into any more purely tea party squabbles re/ literary merit

especially of those writers who have no interest in conserving our heritage or who consistently avoid establishing facts of our history.

After all there are several vols/ of my literery criticism from which you could attain yr/ own conclusions as to my interest both in language and ethics.

pardon the augustan phrasing

banzai

and campa cavallo

yrs.

E. P.

If you want a nice afternoon at yr/ discussion circle I suggest a study of the mendacities *persisted* in by most of our journalists

and the efforts, dating back to 1913 or

even to such estimable characters as dear old G. K. C (hesterton) to get off one's job onto otiose discussion.

no malice on G. K. C's part, just the drift.

Start with the suppression of the record of Antonious Pius. and go on to King James the worst.

Yeats the only one of yr/ ball team that didn't shudder at the idea that damage might be done to his ignorance.

Sandbag worse than Frost because he pretends to write history.

During the course of one visit I asked Pound if he was pleased that the young, advancing poets were returning to lyricism. He did not seem much interested in this turn of the conversation, but did say: "Yes, the ashcan has no superiority over the rose in my cosmos." Once when he was in especially good spirits I named a few names. "Dylan Thomas," he said, "is not my cup of tea. I thought I had done with Lowells after Amy, but Robert came to see me several times. He is probably the best poet and the best human value in the U.S." Then, almost as if to himself, "I never met a poet I didn't like, if I liked his poetry. A good poet has to have character."

He rarely talked about his association with Radio Rome, but he did say: "I never would have broadcast if Senator [Burton K.] Wheeler hadn't told me F. D. R. was seizing autocratic power. I did not betray my country. I never renounced my citizenship. Hiss, a proven traitor, is out and making $12,000 a year."

I usually brought along candy or cake, which the poet passed around among other visitors, or put aside for them. When I commented on the fact that he rarely touched the sweets, he said he tried not to eat rich food, for it gave him too much energy. He added that while he was in the "gorilla cage" at Pisa they fed him like an animal, but he ate little, and for the same reason.

As part of my campaign I had asked a number of newspaper friends to write stories and editorials on the Pound case. The most effective response was an editorial by James J. Kilpatrick, brilliant and courageous editor of the *Richmond News-Leader*. Since this was widely circulated I quote it in full:

From the *Richmond News-Leader*
February 7, 1958

Ezra Pound: Set Him Free!
[*An Editorial*]

Last April, this newspaper urged editorially that proceedings be instituted by the Department of Justice aimed at releasing Ezra Pound from the lunatic asylum to which this aging poet is now confined in Washington.

Since then other events have occurred that serve to emphasize, however irrelevantly, the bitter injustice of the treatment imposed upon Pound. We have in mind, of course, the Supreme Court's decision in the Watkins case, and the subsequent release from custody of Communist subversives by the dozen.

This was the sin of Ezra Pound, that 15 years ago, while in Italy, he made some propaganda broadcasts for the Fascist government urging Americans not to support the war effort. The effect of these broadcasts, it may reasonably be assumed, was nil or near it. Yet in 1945 he was brought back to the United States, indicted for treason, and brought on to trial. In February of 1946, he was certified as insane and hustled off to St. Elizabeths Hospital. He has been there ever since. The indictment is still pending.

It is not for Pound the individual, nor for Pound the poet, that we revive this plea for his release. We never met the old gentleman, and we can't understand his poetry. But if there is any justice or mercy under heaven, then justice and mercy demand his freedom.

Is Pound insane? He is certainly no more insane than other poets and intellectuals whose eccentricities and obscurities are not thought dangerous to the public. We have seen some of Pound's letters, written within the past month. Odd, yes; obscene, yes; bitter, yes; but lunatic? Pooh! The files of this office bulge with letters from correspondents, all walking the streets of Richmond as free men, reflecting aberrations and psychoses more strange than any that afflict Mr. Pound.

Ezra Pound will be 73 this year. He has not much life left in him. Since he was incarcerated 12 years ago, the United States government has forgiven every other enemy of World War II. We have embraced the Germans, rebuilt Japan, re-established relations with Italy. Our only enemies today are the Communists, whom Pound cordially detests, and now even the Communists —avowed, open, arrogant agents of Russian imperialism are turned loose from jails to do their worst.

No possible useful purpose is served by keeping Pound locked up in St. Elizabeths. To all intents and purposes, he remains a political prisoner—in a nation that prides itself on political freedom. What does it take to get him free?

JAMES J. KILPATRICK

I gave this editorial the widest possible distribution, sending a copy to, among others, Mr. MacLeish. He replied: "Much obliged. I sent it along to a certain spot in Washington where I thought it might do the most good."

(10)

13 Nov (1957)

DEAR H. M.

Re/ your suggestion that I write a letter to "some" paper. Can you get the general reason why this does NOT appear to me useful. Maybe some interest in Horton's unsuccessful attempt to get TIME to correct a lie, Horton having two witnesses to the falsehood.

I don't think you can show any connection between my telling Kasper to read Confucius and Agassiz and his present imprisonment.

AND obviously the heroism of a Crommelyn is much more stimulating to youth than the doctrines of moderation.

Does yr/ good brother keep his readers alerted to proved and provable activity of subversives,
    certain events in Arlington do not seem to have been of strictly local origin.
    I am in no position to judge particular local events
                            and do not think I
have ever formed judgements on them.

The total decay of education in the U. S. is no more flagrent than in neglect of the opening chapter of vol SECOND of Coke's Institutes.
    there shd/ be NO college degree given without basic knowledge of the parts of Coke and Blackstone which concern EVERYBODY
    not merely lawyers engaged in technicalities.

Yrs
E. POUND

(11)

17 Nov (1957)

DEAR H. M.

I should be very much interested to know what news you have had from General [J. F. C.] Fuller[5] and Admiral Sir Barry Domvile.[6]

Have you sent me Mr. Kilpatrick's editorial?

I have been arguing with W. C. Williams and the great Marianne for some years. Both of them have made remarks in public, Marianne in Dec. Esquire fairly emphatic.
    Williams BASICLY muddled about a number of things, but never has written a line merely to get money.

MacLeish I am in correspondence with, Frost I have not been in contact with for over 40 years.

Sandburg emitted some pity on TV a couple of weeks ago.

Also the term "commands space." My son-in-law has discovered that the parts of his articles (mainly on Egyptology, but not shunning vital facts re/ the administration of the Pharoahs) that are "OMITTED for lack of space" are always the SAME things, i.e. the parts that touch on matters which worry the crablice and fomentors of international strife and internal corruption. Your last letter is undated, but seems to have been sent before you had seen the December "Esquire."

the definition which several of the benevolent writers have given of their own mental equipments is VERY interesting, but this is no time for me to annoy them/

and if they persist in maintaining ignorance of factual detail, I can only wait for the diminution of the general public intelligence.

p. 219 Catherine [Drinker] Bowen's "The Lion and the Throne" has the following quote.

"When one knoweth of any treason or felony and concealith it," Coke later wrote, "this is misprision of treason, the offender to be imprisoned for life, to forfeit all his goods, debts and duties forever, and the profits of his lands during his life." Coke adds that "by the common law, concealment of high treason was treason." This re/trial of Walter Raleigh.

General del Ville[7] is on record that what I did was for the good of the country.

I haven't asked your opinion of how much good it does the U. S. to have Russia sprawled into Berlin and over half of civilized Europe.

Anyhow the stuff in Esquire will interest you. Dec. issue. Also one good letter in the November issue, by Mrs. Reid.

at any rate, although Birmingham is no longer editor of the paper, it wd/ appear that he certainly was not fired for printing Rovere's article.

Not that they have corrected some of the errors IN that article. Although Rovere's attention has been directed to the main one/ fact being printed in the N. [ew] Directions paper back selected poems/ and in the British Who's Who.

which several of the professors still ignore in their correspondence.

Is ANYone in this country old enough or possessed memory enough to remember Romain Rolland's activity from 1914/ 19, from Switzerland "Au dessus du conflit."?

Answer I had from an english visitor yesterday: No, I was born in 1913. I was an infant at that time.

Whom did I tell a few days ago that at any rate Agassiz and Confucius haven't been blamed for Gov. Faubus.

At any rate Giovannini's letter is printed in Esquire, but you may have missed it as it is on p. 52/ 54

What do you know about P. M. Malin?

                          he repeats a certain amount of tommy rot, picked up from what I suppose is his usual source of information, the idiot press.

Cordially yours

E. POUND

In the foregoing, Pound refers to Carl Sandburg's "Meet The Press Interview," on N.B.C. on October 27, 1957, in which he said, among other things, "I'm sorry for Ezra but I go on reading him and will as long as I live. . . ." Perhaps the most interesting reference in the November 17 letter is to Catherine Drinker Bowen's *The Lion and the Throne*, for it was in this book that he met Sir Edward Coke (1552-1634), English jurist, later Lord Chief Justice, and best known for his four *Institutes*. As to the Coke quote, Pound thought President Roosevelt was a traitor, so for him to have kept quiet would have been "misprision of treason" that is, "concealment of, or omission to notify the authorities of, treason."

Pound was highly pleased that Kilpatrick supported efforts to gain his freedom. In fact, the editorial formed the basis for an enduring friendship. Nonetheless, the poet insisted on getting the facts straight and no doubt expressed himself strongly on the point of accuracy when displaying the editorial to friends. As a result, one of them wrote to me about "serious misstatements of fact." I answered, in part, "If there is one thing Mr. Pound needs it is a friendly press. The tone of the editorial was altogether friendly and called for Mr. Pound's release. What good purpose would be served by digging into the bowels of the Italian fiasco? Rather than correct Mr. Kilpatrick I would urge Mr. Pound to write him a letter thanking him for the editorial and the stand he has taken. I think it is tremendously important that we forget things that have no direct bearing on Mr. Pound's release and do all we can to add to the reservoir of good will which seems to be rising daily. . . ."

(12)

22 Nov 1957

DEAR H. M.

Thanks very much for the enclosures, especially the two letters. I had not seen the *News Leader* editorial, so you must have omitted it from some earlier letter in which you thought it had been enclosed.

I certainly never heard of it last April. IF I had answered every misstatement made in the past 40 and more years, there wd/ be no poetry for your society to disagree about.

One of the enemies' potent weapons is that of getting men's minds off their proper work.

The errors in the *Richmond News* [*Leader*] COULD be belatedly corrected, without anyone's sticking their neck out.

I was not (vid. Gen. Fuller as corroboration) sending axis propaganda.

IF the *Richmond News Leader* wants facts, I could find someone to supply, let us say, 4 or 5, not burden their space.

There was NO testimony given in court, so that their April notice is misleading.

There was already testimony offered in Rome and refused, and as I recall, the indictment gave no instance of treasonable WORDS, but merely gathered technicians to assert that I had spoken on the radio/

which I had never denied. I had insisted that I spoke AS AN AMERICAN, who had been given freedom of microphone and whose transmissions would not be suggested to him by anyone else and shd/ not be contrary to his conscience or to his duties as an AMERICAN citizen.

Two recent inquiries, one from a man named John Colombo and another named John Wilcocks.

I do not know how you gave Domvile the idea that I would not go to Italy? or where you collected it.

It is hard for me to think that any man, even a burocrat wd/ at this time try to impose conditions re/ where I wd/ live.

Borah said he couldn't see what a man like me would find to DO here.

Certainly my daughter and grandchildren WANT me back in Italy, & I don't know of any stronger pull in any other direction. I should like to see Brazil, and once hoped to see the Altar of Heaven

but that part of China is rather outside the UN limits just now.

I should think some people wd PREFER to have me safe in the Tirolo

ad interim, cordially yrs

EP

As to criminals being terrified of what I might say, my testimony could hardly carry weight at this late date, and the surviving villains are so old that they wd/ be dead before it could effect them.

I had sent the Pounds a Smithfield ham for Christmas, and had it cooked in Richmond, feeling sure no one in Washington would have any idea how to prepare it.

(13)

S. LIZ   18 Dec 1957

TO H. M.

with season's greetings.

I understand that a HAM has arrived at Brother's Place.

presuming that it is as specified, and in accord with past performances of the State of Va. I refrain from further comment until I can attest from personal experience the quality as well as the quidity of the festive donation.

Cordially yrs,

E.P.

I take it you are not trying to rent house property in Richmond or revive the intentions of Mr. Jefferson in regard to yr/ state University. Roanoke WAS a bit removed from the teeming activities of the metropolis etc. Tucker, as you may recall, brought out an edition of Blacksone (J. R [andolph's] step-father) did I mention the familial connection.

The ham arrived safely—just as I was re-reading W. H. Hudson's "My Friend the Pig."
D.P. [ound]

(14)

31 Dec 57

H. M.

Monsieur Horton having sliced that HAM and delivered a reasonable amount of same in condition to be attacked locally, let me

STATE: THAT HAM is kulchur, THAT ham is civilization.

any service I can perform to or for the hamists I will endeaver to purrForm.

Sorry I can't see yr/ friends whoever, but their letter came after I had got the Thursday or whatever absoLOOTly crammed,

hope it will occur some other time,
besides their agenda was not re/ anything that demands haste.

best for '58

E.P.

(15)

1 Jan 58

H. M.

Further development / having TASTED the said ham, curiousity arises.

How can Monsieur Horton OBtain another specimen of same? ?

Marcella avers that Mrs. H COOKed the ham

I AM

as the wops say, in forse,

as to whether sd/ HAM was already cooked on arrival/

This is a mere trivial detail, or not as the case may be/,

it does matter whether those not in the possession of suitable machinery may attempt to DEAL with the hind quarter of porker/

There is NO doubt that the Washington OUTLET can be widened.

enquiringly yrs

E.P.

4 devotees ready to

issue proclamations

declHAMations.

It was characteristic of Pound that he wanted to infuse everything that interested him with his tremendous drive and genius. This had been the pattern of his life, and it had made him the editor of the twentieth century. The poet had always looked down on poetry societies as carry-overs from the Genteel Tradition of the nineteenth century. Since I was

president of The Poetry Society of Virginia, talk naturally
turned to our efforts to enlarge the audience for poetry and
to encourage young writers.

As I told him about bringing George Garrett, Peter
Viereck, Richard Wilbur, Donald Hall, Louis Simpson,
Peter Kane Dufault, and other young, advancing poets to
read for Virginia audiences, he realized we had got away
from the cup-and-saucer sort of thing. He took it upon himself to tell me how we could best serve the Muse.

(16)

2 Feb 1958

IMPERSONAL MEMORANDUM TO H. M.

Standing above petty squabbles of 3rd rate writers etc/ and not
tied by the Chicago gang/ The Va. Poetry Soc. COULD undertake
some functions that most writers are too squirrel-headed to consider.

The tax system is total imbecility and infamy/ I can't go into
that now, and it would be untimely for me, in particular, to start
a general squawk on the subject. At this particular moment.

BUT as they are fools enough to swallow the root of the evil, all
one can do is to try clipping branches, and a poetry soc. is ideal
place to start.

A writer should not be TAXED on his gross receipts.[8] He has
BUSINESS expenses.

1. Typing
2. Books necessary for his work. If
he does any work and don't merely flutter.
3. Travel expenses if he lectures, the
lecturer more likely to think of practical measures.

The enemies of mankind might be induced to allow tax deduction
on 1, 2 and
4. Stationary, high price of carbon
paper etc.

The professoriat is very weak on professional honor and solidarity,
a society concerned

not only with rivals productions but with the product
                                    might move toward greater
coherence/ AND intercommunication between those who alledg-
edly, by their profession (teaching the humanities) claim to
HAVE read something.

Yr/ governor is having a culture-fund or something, etc. is he
INTERested in what is actually taught

EITher to white or afro-saxons?

Yrs   E. POUND

(17)

9 February 58

DEAR MEACHAM

As D. P. was ill, I only saw your letter of the 5th. after you
had left, when I looked at the papers Marcella had brought on
from D. P.

Partia Mia was, as you may know held up 38 years since when I
have thought more about HOW you can deal with arts, poetry
included.

Indubitably professional honor is a help. Not "WE WANT" but
as Q. Eliz. emended in letter of Coke's appointment. NOT for the
Queen but for TRUTH.

Juries of selection tend to eliminate the finest sensibility of the
best juror.

The best I have found as solution is that the selection should be
made by INDIVIDUALS,
    different individuals,
                                    if there are to be three awards, let
three different qualified "judges" select one contestant apiece.

That wd/ give say Frost's preference, my preference, or even X's
preference.

                                    and the desire to get a better
representative of each point of view wd/ put each selector on his
mettle.

The chance of something GOOD getting an award? I got $50 from Trenton[9] BiCentennial

but I sent in a ms/ only because there were to be TEN awards
being perfectly
certain I wd/ not be either first, 2nd, or probably even 5th.

I have never reprinted
the poem, but may sometime do so for the sake of what I was
aiming at, and possibly one good line.[10] [Ernst Friedrich] Richter
in his books on Harmony and Counterpoint says: These are the
laws of Harmony and Counterpoint. They have NOTHING to do
with composition, which is a very different kind of activity.

Homer is not immoral or even amoral. But the occidental tradition
is rather of entertainment than of construction.

The chinese definately from Confucius Anthology, have had a
tradition that the ODES ought to make MEN (and ladies).

Good fences/good neighbors/ may be the poetry socs/wd get
higher % of results if they put more emphasis on the good life,
and composition of society   Poetry having

a function in it. NOT expecting the poets to accept and boost
some particular patent medicine, but having at least a velleity
toward health and hilarity (in the theological sense).

Herewith the Connecticut Charter /

What did the VA. Poetry Soc/ do when the state was celebrating
the VA/ Bill of Rights, or whatever?

And thank your friend for his editorial.

Yrs   EP

What do you know of Cudworth Flint, and the Va/ Quarterly?
I hadn't heard of the magazine for years. Thanks for copy.

Cudworth Flint was, at the time of this letter, Chairman of
the English Department at Dartmouth College. The *Virginia
Quarterly Review*, founded in 1925, is edited by Miss Charlotte Kohler whom Pound was to meet while he was my
guest in Richmond.

(18)

(undated)

DEAR H.M.

Just heard Senator Kerr on wave length 1390 dont know if it reaches Richmond,

but yr/ friend on the News Leader might have enjoyed it. Re/ Andy Jackson etc.

seemed to me to tie in with yr impression of what was needed on Friday.

At any rate cant do any harm for News Leader to know what Kerr was hammering on.

I suppose the text or tape recording could be found for him.

No need to mix it with any other topic, or personal angle whatever.

Yrs   E. P.

p.s. Monday/

re/ poetry societies, prizes, etc.

certain kinds of common sense and decency have been so ridiculed, after puritan excess, Comstockery, etc. that no one dares to mention 'em.

For poetry contests, the old fashioned method of demanding a poem on a theme, i.e. about something, has its merits.

Bill of Rights celebration for example, gave a chance, I don't know if it was taken.

after Freud and 1917, education to make character got a black eye.

Monsignor Spence was on TV about text books, whether he wd/ really back any serious effort re/ contents of 'em is another matter.

at any rate a few people are beginning to notice the boycott of american tradition and substitution of Pinkosity.

For theme subjects / Andy Jackson, character of General Lee, sam houston, much better than analyzing their own bellyaches,

Muses "daughters of Memory"/ let them write about something WORTH remembering. get a little education into 'em SOMHOW.

P.S. 11 Feb/ for long range, impersonal action. What does Dun
& Bradstreet know of Prentice Hall, Englewood N. J./ which
apparently publishes BOOKS, text books, in quantity. An approach
from business NON-egg-head angle, might have good effect. mass
production of print.

(19)

S. ELIZ   Marzo 1958

Yes, of course Governor A [lmond]/ could be of immense use.
ANY man in public life who will examine any idea seriously is of
enormous value.

I suggest you take the line, or quote from Va./ Quarterly or
Richmond Daily./

a nazi, a bolchevik or even a pinko has the right to have his ideas
examined ONE AT A TIME.

Cyril Clemens has been in again, and is talking to people/ he is
a wholesome influence.

I suppose you know his *Mark Twain Quarterly*. Thanks for
the last batch of interior decorations.[11]

E. P.

Any use to say that I do not have ideas/ only a belief that certain
facts should be supplied to people to prevent their getting FALSE
notions.

In the following letter the poet comments on a letter I had
written to the *Washington Star*, which the newspaper published, much to Pound's surprise. The tide of favorable
public opinion was running full. Letters were reaching the
Attorney General from poets and other prominent citizens
from all over the country, and MacLeish was winning his
titanic struggle against inertia, timidity, and prejudice in high
places.

Since Pound seemed to enjoy the *Virginia Quarterly Review*, I suggested that he send one of the unpublished cantos

to the editor. I felt this was a good place for him to appear in print, and also a good time. To those who do not know Pound personally, and do not understand his attitude toward his own poetry, portions of the following letter will come as a surprise.

The public mask of Ezra Pound was often belligerent and disputatious, but the face he turned to friends and struggling writers was altogether different, as these letters bear witness. Eliot said, "No one could have been kinder to young men and to writers who seemed worthy and unrecognized." The fact that Pound was always modest about his own poetry is supported by the following letter:

(20)

19 Marzo 58

DEAR H.M.

Thanks for excellent letter to the Star/ whether it gets past their cawpy desk or not.

Also thanks re/ Va. Quarterly/ which MAY need a bit of sales talk from you when they get the ms/ in answer to their letter.

> The Rev. Moelwyn Merchant
> 15 Archer Road
> Penarth, Glamorgam
> Wales, British Isles

will tell 'em how important it is. Distinguished Shakespearian scholar, ref/ Folger lie/bury etc,

It (Canto 99) is gist of the Emperor Yong Ching on the Sacred Edict. etc.

they only need 4 ideograms/ and the Canto is fairly self contained/ which many of 'em are not.

It dont need a lot of familiarity with the rest of the poem/ tho the last three Chinese cantos, 59/61 lead up to it.

Yrs

E. P.

Excellent photo of you/ never seen a better of anyone as likeness.

(21)

1 April (but as of the 2nd.)

DEAR H. M.

I hope to see Kilpatrick sometime, and to discuss serious, but impersonal matters with him. But it would come pretty close to violating a sort of general understanding not to deal with newspaper men if I approached him at this particular time.

I dont know who was being heckled on TV (Huntley Outlook) sunday but he was a fine old chap[12] who had resigned from Boston Latin school in disgust at the decay of education

and Wyllie may know who he is,
                                    I am trying to find out
whether the Va. ¼ly ascends to Parnassus at a bound, or NOT, some use should be made of this man, the first clear, and I mean VERY clear, diagnosis of what is wrong
    AND something that can perfectly well be remedied.
                                    Perhaps Wyllie
wd/ like to hear from me on this subject.

Hammarskjöld is busy with more IMMEDiate crises, pretty much every week or so. I don't think I should abuse his good will. At any rate do thank Kilpatrick, and send me a few WHOLE copies of his paper, to think about,
                    NOT merely from personal angle.

                                    Ever yours,

                                    EZRA POUND

P.S. Olivia Rossetti Agresti says she is sending me two more installments of her memoirs. I don't know whether you saw some of them in *Edge*. But Stock is leaving Australia, *Edge* is suspended. Would the Va. ¼ly be interested in seeing the ms, when I get it?

(22)

Apr [1958]

H. M.

    Va. Quarterly heard from.

Just what USE is being made of the stables at Monticello?? I liked the look of Charlottesville in 1939

Yrs

E. P.

On several occasions Pound spoke warmly of Monticello and said he would like to live on the grounds. He seems now to have settled on the stables. His reference to curricula in the following was prompted by a speech I had sent him, "The Battle of the Curriculum," delivered before the Oklahoma Adult Education Association on January 7, 1958 by C. Scott Fletcher, at that time president of The Fund For Adult Education. It was his thesis that liberal education is continuing education. "Most adults," he says, "think of adult education as an activity mildly embarrassing. . . . The view of continuing education as remedial is based on the misconception that education is a concluded achievement rather than an endless process." Education for citizenship is emphasized throughout the speech.

"StringBeanFellow" is Stringfellow Barr, onetime president of St. John's College, Annapolis, Maryland, and one of the originators of the One Hundred Great Books Program.

(23)

(*undated*)

DEAR H. M.

Excellent news re/ action re/ CURRICULA.
BUT absolute mistrust of "best books" if you mean the St. John's ONE HUNDRED,

or any
similar collection of famous books selected MERELY to provide a forest or morass in which the student is lost or swamped.

Believe StringBeanFellow has since
turned
against Beanery slush. but have no details.

The Sq. $/ is the ONLY series aimed at education.

I suggest that you write to Catherine D. Bowen for help to get the Sq/ INTO high sch/ and colleges AT ONCE.

Address 921 Mt. Pleasant Road, Bryn Mawr, Pa.

and no secret that her two books, John Adams, and "Lion and Throne" (re/ Coke) are worth more than all the damn pseudo history now taught in the beaneries,
                                                              so far as
I can make out.

The National Review is improving/ note letter from Cookson on Kenner's objection to phoney history in current issue.

A.S.C. prof. has just sent in 11 pages of extracts from Forrestal's Diary. I don't know that Va. ¼ly wd/ be interested.
In fact you might find out not where they ARE at this moment, but what they WANT to be and do,

   this is easier in conversation than by letter. No use in asking people to send in what Miss Kohler don't want.

Am strong believer in having an editorial program, whether communicated to anyone outside the office or not.

                              saves people kidding themselves.

How far is the Va. ¼ly an Almond[13] review ??

Given that title it OUGHT to be Virginian, not even damn yankee.

                                   or midwestern egg head

Just recd/ lousy circular from Univ of Chi. Press.

I dont suppose Va. ¼ly printed Hammarskjöld's speech at celebration of Va. bill of rights. but did they even notice it?

VA ¼ly of course should be the main vortex for all the South.

   Any good research work on the Lees (1776 Lees)
Mrs. Bowen don't know of any recent work on them.

What do you know of the violent southern states press assn/ ? purports to print in D. C. but their paper arrived here from Chicago seems to count of Chicago Tribune.

Ad interium

E. P.

Thanks for identifying Marston/ are they getting him for the ¼ ly?

The "group or vortex" referred to in the following letter consisted of James J. Kilpatrick, editor of the *Richmond News-Leader;* John Cook Wyllie, Librarian, University of Virginia; and Miss Charlotte Kohler, editor, the *Virginia Quarterly Review.* The "G" is Fred Grab, young friend of Pound's who accompanied him to Richmond, much to everyone's surprise.

(24)

13 Ap [1958]

Dear H. M.

The status of any REVIEW depends on the degree of awareness in the central office.

Even if the VIEWS of the edt/ board are deader than mutton/
so long as they
are clearly defined, the Review serves to enlighten.

Even Eliot with his absurd program is useful because he gives one something solid to stand AGAINST.

With yr Editor (R. News L/r), librarian and edt. Va. ¼ly you have a group or vortex,
probably not opportune to take the more
active label.

You may as well know without delay that there are three writers whom I respect.

Rock,[14] Goullart[15] and Mrs. [Catherine Drinker] Bowen.

You waste energy talking about "poetry" UNless you specify that merely writing verse

with LESS knowledge and sincerity than you demand of a prose writer is NO answer,

and the tolerance of slop IN "Poetry" is the root cause of its getting shoved into
subsidiary position
        as "filler"
                to eliminate "printer's fat" as blank
spaces on pages are, or were called in England.

You ought to back Ph. Marson to the FULL and AT ONCE
        no sense in delay
he diagnoses the syphilis in our educ/
                        due possibly to Vienna
and Moscow.

No foreign born kikietrist has done ANYthing toward developing civic sense in this country.

they ought all to be examined on basis of what is, in the money press, called "background" /

(or so a european correspondent observes in a recent letter.)

I only saw Grab for a few minutes, but expect him back. He evidently has broken into the A [ssociated] P [ress] BUT he ought to be useful both to Kilpatrick and the Va ¼ly.

Not too many Y [oung] M [en] can give you direct report on Shanghai, Bassra, Beirut, Bombay.

Is it against the U. S. paideuma to issue manifestos??

No, damn it, the Dec. of Ind. and the BL of rts/ were manifestos.

Only in decay did the custom wane.
You will notice that the Imagist manifesto got thru one helluva lot more than [Ford Madox] Ford's
gentle meander of "Impressions and Memories."

Marston has most brilliantly DIAGnosed the pest.

the remedy is as
simple as cutting out a diseased appendix.

Simple and surgical.
AT *the right point*, i.e. college entrance requirements.

Two languages, at least one inflected.

mathematics, algebra and plane geometry. More if you
   like, but at least geometry/
                                   and freshmen OBLIGED to
take analytics,

   U.S. History, not Toqueville and Sandbag/ but J. Adams, B.
Adams. Van Buren, Benton, Del Mar.

That wd/ kill the god damn spewdeal pro moscow Mrs. O. R.
and the lot of 'em.

Will you, preferably with the four of you all at once, consider
these points,
                                         If you can't
get yr three friends altogether, chaw on it seriatim.
                           and make sure all three under-
stand it/

   whether they want to put it into manifesto form.
                           you cd/ get some damn good profs to
sign it.

   List of possible signers if you want it

                        ever yrs/

and again, this "best books" / NOT the St. John, Stringbean 100,
and not too much fat a la Montaigne

                                            EP

   This little volume is not the place, nor am I the writer,
to deal with the Pound *paideia* (educational method). This
must be left to the professoriate, which I respect as much
as Pound detests, yet any careful reader familiar with the
writings of the poet will know that Pound borrowed *Paideuma*
from Frobenius, German archeologist and anthropologist, "as
a word not current for the express purpose of scraping off the
barnacles . . . of a long used term," and he uses it "for the
gristly roots of ideas that are in action."[16] This concept is
at the heart of Pound's thought, and it is developed in all his
writings, prose and poetry, including the letters in this

volume, and all his correspondence through the years—and it runs like a golden thread through the *Cantos*.

In writing and talking about the deficiencies in our curricula he often complained that his generation grew up in "black ignorance of economics" especially monetary economics, and he emphasizes the importance of money in history. Dudley Fitts, in his review of *Impact*,[17] a collection of Pound's essays edited by Noel Stock, says the poet's educational method "is a system of lucid shocks, sharp and disparate perceptions and revelations." This system would not have worked with average students in a junior college—or average students anywhere, for that matter, but I believe Pound was concerned with education for the élite, and so he assumed, with Robespierre, that light footprints are enough for a keen eye.

In a letter to Professor Felix E. Schelling of the University of Pennsylvania,[18] Pound proposed a fellowship for creative ability, "regardless of whether the men had any university degrees whatever." Dr. Schelling replied with what Pound regarded as the epitaph for the American university system: "The university is not here for the exceptional man." "It does not matter," Pound says, "whether you load up your memory with the chronological sequence of what has happened, or the names of protagonists, or authors of books . . . so long as you understand the process now going on, enveloping you as an individual, in a social order." He quotes an author from "I have forgotten what book," and adds, parenthetically and significantly, "Knowledge is not culture. The domain of culture begins when one has 'forgotten what book'."[19]

In his letters to me and in our conversations (or monologues) as well as in his correspondence with friends throughout his long life, he is often preoccupied with the failure of the American educational system, and here, as in everything he touched, he became involved. We do not teach history properly; students should study at least two foreign languages, one inflected; and he deplores our failure to recognize, as Confucius did, that the process of learning and teaching stimulate one another. "I always wonder," he wrote Dr. Schelling, "when the creative element will be recognized; when the mind of the student is to be recognized as at least potentially dynamic and not wholly as a receptacle."[20]

On teaching poetry he has this to say: "For practical contact with all past poetry that was actually sung in its day I suggest that each dozen universities combine in employing a couple of singers who understand the meaning of words. A half-dozen hours spent in listening to the lyrics actually performed would give the student more knowledge of melopoeia than years of work in philology."[21]

Pound returns again and again to another of his preoccupations—the failure of American universities to encourage students to seek the precise word, *le mot juste*. "Language is the main means of human communication. If an animal's nervous system does not transmit sensations and stimuli the animal atrophies. If a nation's literature declines, the nation atrophies and decays."[22]

In his essay "How to Read"[23] Pound suggests a "definite curriculum in place of the present *emiettements* . . . a curriculum for instructors, for obstreperous students who wish to annoy dull instructors, for men who haven't had time for systematized college courses." This includes, among others, Confucius, Homer, Ovid, a Provençal Song Book, Dante and his circle, Villon, Voltaire, Stendhal, Flaubert, Gautier, Corbière, and Rimbaud. "After this inoculation the student could be with safety exposed to modernity or anything else in literature." Pound added later to his curriculum six titles of the Square Dollar Series: (1) *The Chinese Written Character as a Medium for Poetry*, by Ernest Fenollosa, and in the same volume, *The Unwobbling Pivot* and *The Great Digest of Confucius*, translated by Ezra Pound; (2) *The Analects of*

Confucius, translated by Ezra Pound; (3) *Gists from Agassiz*, selected by John Kasper; (4) *Barbara Villiers*, by Alexander Del Mar; (5) *Bank of the United States*, by Thomas H. Benton; and (6) *Roman and Moslem Money*, by Alexander Del Mar.

The account of all the activities in Pound's behalf will, like his definitive biography, be written in a later generation, and it has seemed to me that those who participated even in a minor way in helping to get the indictments dropped have an obligation to tell as best they can what happened—who did what and when—and then leave interpretations to those who come after.

There are many who feel that, however wrong-minded Pound was, he was subjected to cruel and unusual treatment, and this number has increased steadily. In his book, *Fair Fights and Foul*,[24] Mr. Thurman Arnold, distinguished attorney who defended Pound at the final hearing wrote, "Yet the philosophical morality that saved Pound from a criminal trial was of little advantage to him as far as confinement was concerned. Had he been tried, his testimony, together with the unintelligible nature of his broadcasts, might have convinced the jury that—insane or not—he did not have the requisite intent to commit treason. Or, if the jury did convict him under these peculiar circumstances, he certainly would not have been given the sentence that he actually served." He goes on to say that "to the increasing horror of the literary world, here and abroad, Pound was detained in the criminal ward of St. Elizabeths for thirteen years."

As I have examined the record of the Pound case, going wherever possible to original sources, I incline more and more to the opinion of Napoleon that history is a myth agreed upon—literary history, at any rate. The myth-maker in the Pound affair was the great poet Robert Frost. He convinced himself that he was the sole architect of Pound's freedom, and it was apparently a simple matter to convince others. In the definitive biography of Frost by Professor Lawrance Thompson (which promises to be the best biography of this century, if the first volume, *Robert Frost, the Early Years*,[25] is a fair sample of what is to come) the author says: "A good raconteur, he usually varied his accounts, and whenever the bare facts troubled him, he discreetly clothed them with fictions. This imaginative process caused him to mingle self-deceptions with little falsehoods; it even caused him gradually to convince himself that some of these fictions were genuine truths."

It is only in the light of Professor Thompson's interpretive biography that Frost's fabrications are understandable. In any event, the myth that Frost was the one person responsible for the poet's release has been reinforced by writers and by others who did not study the case, and so, having cast Pound as the villain, Frost was to be the hero. It is easy to see why this is so. In the first place, it was a simple explanation, easily grasped, and Frost had become the great Father Figure, the all-wise, who traveled around the country tickling the groundling's ears and playing to the hilt the role of benign farmer-poet.

In interviews and lectures during the period when Pound was still news, Frost played up his role and played down what others had done. On the evening of the day Pound was released, Frost read some of his poems in New York City. After he had been called back by the ovation (richly deserved, for here was a great poet reading deathless poetry—I once spent two nights on a train to hear him read for an hour) he said, "This morning's paper said I took two years to get Ezra Pound out of jail [*sic*] but the truth is I did it all in just one week." On May 22, 1958, he told Carter Barber of the *Los Angeles Times*, "Magnanimity was the thing about getting Ezra out of jail. . . . Archie MacLeish was trying for a long time. No luck. Well, I happened to be in Washington and said I would try. Archie had just about

given up." After establishing his central role in the reporter's
mind, he added, "there were only three people of any importance in the case, Rogers, Arnold, and Overholser."

Almost every book I have read about Pound that in any
way touches on the tragic events at St. Elizabeths, including
volumes by the two lawyers in the case,[26] accepts and thus
reinforces the Frost myth, with one important exception, and
that is the account by the man who knows Frost better than
any man living. In *Selected Letters of Robert Frost*, Lawrance
Thompson[27] says so many men of letters and statesmen had
brought so much pressure to bear on the Department of
Justice that Pound would have been released when he was
even if Frost had never entered the picture.

Frost did play an important role towards the end, however reluctantly he performed, and he deserves full credit for
it, but it is necessary to see his role in proper perspective.
The "Swinger of Birches" must wait in the wings. He will
make his dramatic appearance in the final moments of the
last act. And he will almost miss his cue.

I was close enough to events to observe much of what
went on, and for the rest I have corresponded with or interviewed most of the key figures. The written record is, in
itself, revealing, if one takes the trouble to read it. In retro-
spect it is clear that, no matter how hard friends and sym-
pathizers worked, they could do nothing until the attitude
of the public changed, and this is what happened, though
slowly. Pound's continued production of original verse and
translations increased his reputation and led to a growing
sense of embarrassment among Americans who had to explain to foreigners why their government had been holding
for so long a time and in an indeterminate status a poet of
international stature. Then there was some squirming and
shifting among intellectuals, which had an immediate effect
on the attitude of the press. Dr. Giovannini has remarked
that when he was gathering material for his paper, "The

Strange Case of Ezra Pound,"[28] he discovered that "the American press had shown no interest in the case of Pound the prisoner, and I had to build my argument largely from statements in the foreign press."

All this seemed to change overnight when the press took notice of Hemingway's plea for Pound's release when he accepted the Nobel Prize for Literature, yet it must have been building up for a long time, compounded of shame, guilt, embarrassment and the realization that perhaps we were wrong in the first place. Whatever the reasons may have been, news media and literary journals decided to have a look at what had been going on at St. Elizabeths. News magazines reported at some length Giovanni Papini's appeal to American traditional toleration of nonconformists, and they also mentioned Professor José Ve de Pina Martins' plea in behalf of Pound, which was delivered over the Vatican radio. Hayden Carruth's article analyzing the poet's career (*Perspectives*, Summer 1956) did much to restore Pound to respectability, as did "The Case of Ezra Pound," by Sam Hynes in *Commonweal* (December 9, 1955). One statement in this latter article was picked up and has been repeated by many who have written about the poet: "The case of Ezra Pound is a significant modern symbol, and it is only prudent that we Americans should from time to time remind ourselves that in one room at St. Elizabeths there is a closet which contains a national skeleton."

While the Department of Justice seemed unaware of this shift, the changing attitude of the people and the press provided a more favorable climate for those who were trying to open the door to Chestnut Ward. I don't know what literary historians and future biographers will say about some of these people, whether they were a help or a hindrance, and one can only guess at their motives. There is the case of David Horton, for example. He was, during these days, a young Washington attorney who often visited the Pounds, and I know he and his wife were a great comfort to the poet. I am convinced that his interest in the Pound case was genuine and unselfish, but he was criticized for some activities which destroyed his usefulness. He was for a time associated with Kasper and was co-editor and one of the publishers of the Square Dollar Series.

Then there was Eustice Mullins, one of Pound's biographers, whose *Mullins on the Federal Reserve* was published by Kasper and Horton. He met Pound while studying at The Institute of Contemporary Arts in Washington, and there was his friend Sheri Martinelli, a gifted painter who became something of a problem. Both were frequent visitors of Pound. According to Mullins, a friend of his, Rex Lampman, had suffered a nervous breakdown and was a patient in the violent ward at St. Elizabeths. He brought Pound and Lampman together and, as Mullins records it in his biography of the poet, it was Lampman, a newspaperman, who interested Congressman Burdick in the case. The only account of this is in Mullins' book. Congressman Burdick said his interest was not in the man but in the thing. "I'm against people being railroaded into insane asylums." However history deals with this group of the poet's young friends (and they're not off to a very good start), there is no question that their frequent presence at St. Elizabeths resulted in much unfavorable publicity, and Ernest Hemingway and others considered them a distinct liability.

In 1961 I decided to record my friendship with Ezra Pound. Since much of our correspondence and many of our conversations turned on affairs at the hospital and efforts to free him, the name of Archibald MacLeish was frequently mentioned. And so for the past five years I have been urging Mr. MacLeish to discuss his role with me, first by letter and later when we were together at the First Annual Poetry Festival at the University of South Florida at Tampa, where he was the guest of honor and principal speaker. He was adamant in refusal. Once in a telephone conversation and later in a note he agreed the story Robert Frost was telling was something less than the whole story, yet he did not feel it was his place to set the record straight. Finally, in the fall of 1966, he reluctantly agreed to let me examine his Pound file at the Library of Congress with the understanding that I was to draw my own conclusions.

I don't know what was going on in Mr. MacLeish's mind, but I suspect he was persuaded to open his files to me when he realized that the mythic account of Frost has been accepted as a historical fact and that the story of Pound's release was no longer a subject of inquiry. His passion for truth must have overcome his excessive modesty. I might add that my account of the long battle to free Pound, written several years before I examined the MacLeish-Pound file, has not changed basically. Details have been added, of course, but I did not have to study a couple of hundred letters in a restricted file to learn that Mr. MacLeish was the irresistible force behind the drive.

Archibald MacLeish is about as close to the complete man as one can find in this automated age. He was born in Illinois in 1892, graduated from Yale in 1915, and after service in World War I received his LL.B. from Harvard in 1919. After practicing law for a short time he turned to poetry and, over the years, he has become a towering figure in the world of letters. He has been awarded three Pulitzer prizes, two for poetry (*Conquistador*, 1933 and *Collected Poems*, 1952) and one for his magnificent drama based on the Book of Job, *J.B.* (1959). He served as Librarian of Congress (1939-45), Assistant Secretary of State (1944-45), and Chairman of the American Delegation to London to draw up the constitution for UNESCO. He was Boylston professor at Harvard (1949-62) and now, in semiretirement, delivers the Robert Frost Lectures at Amherst.

Mr. MacLeish has known Ezra Pound for almost half

a century, going back to the Paris of the 1920's, and while they had gone their separate ways, they remained united by the bonds of mutual respect and affection. And so it was to MacLeish that Pound and his friends turned less than two weeks after Ezra's arrest on May 5, 1945; first came T. S. Eliot and, later, Ernest Hemingway, Dag Hammarskjöld, and, at the last, Robert Frost, who did what he did at the behest of MacLeish.

On May 16, 1945 Eliot cabled MacLeish: "Just returned from Paris. Anxious to do everything possible to mitigate treatment Ezra Pound. Please advise me." This was followed by a letter in which he said he relied on MacLeish to let him know, ". . . if it appears that there is anything I can do here in his favor, for instance, in the way of enlisting poets and men of letters." He went on to say that he had discussed the case with many people, including members of the armed forces: "I have not heard a single voice express any desire except that Pound should be let off as lightly as possible, and that the whole affair might be forgotten as quickly as possible." On October 17, 1945, in the first letter I have seen written by Pound from the Disciplinary Training Center, he addressed his attorneys in London, stating his case clearly and succinctly, and asking them to arrange for him to see Archibald MacLeish as soon as he reached the United States. Included in this business-like letter was the following touching personal note: "Dorothy visited me a few days ago and brought the good news of Omar. I am very much pleased with his independence and initiative in all ways."

While MacLeish and Pound's other old friends kept in touch with him—William Carlos Williams, Marianne Moore, Louis Zukofsky, T. S. Eliot, E. E. Cummings, and Conrad Aiken to name but a handful, and his newfound champions, G. Giovannini and Craig La Drière who went to St. Elizabeths almost weekly—the mood of the country was not

Dear Harry

Thank god
you are
coming thru
yr. operation.

E

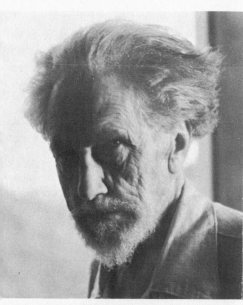

Ezra Pound in 1965

Meacham.

Than. a

as to %

POlit.cal significance

of yr. choice of colour ?

in excitable segment

of Europe. !!

every

E.P.

Thank you also for
Heritage s.
Greetings D.P.

24 th Sept . later

ear H.M.

          Re/ one of yr/ questions . I don't see that it is
ayone's damn business WHAT i wd/ do IF I got out.

, is unConfucian to make plans for circumstances that cannot
alculated.

, would depend on HOW I got out.

s I always spoke as an american , FOR the Constitution , etc.
 wd/ be a joke of jokes to get out ON CON<u>DITION</u> that I returr
 Italy.

would naturally prefer to go live with my daughter to stayin
 the bughouse.

'ter all Borah did say : Waaaal, I'm sure ⊥ don't know
at a man like you would find to DO here ?   ·|

·d knows I can see PLENTY that needs doing.   HERE.

ID the present state of Italy is no picnic , the place has
en largely ruined by two of the greatest HH shits mankind
s known, Roosevelt and Churchill , and even Churchill
nted to attack thru the Balkans so as to save a little
vilization. AND that would not have brough the rHHHNH russian
vages into Europe.

               etc.

                    cordially yours. I will add reflections)
 they occur to me.

 1939 I had got my affairs into enough order so that I was
anning to spend about two months of the year IN the U.S.

 one could have got into a taxi in Rapallo and gone on ooard at
noa. and the Rex wd/ have brought one in 5 days to N.York.

31 Dec 57

EZRA POUND

H.M.

Monsieur Horton having sliced that HAM
and delivered a reasonable amount of same in
condition to be attacked locally. let me STATE :

THAT HAM is kulchur , THAT ham is civilization.
                                    or for
          any service I can perform to the
hamists I will endeavour to purrform.

Sorry I can't see yr/ friends whoever, but their
letter came after I had got the Thursday or whatev
whatever abSoLOOTly crammed,

                         hope it can occur some
other time ,
              besides their agenda was
not re/ anything that demands haste.

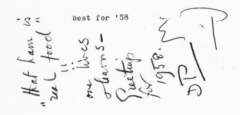

          best for '58

          i Jan 58

EZRA POUND

H M
     Further deVelopment / having TASTED the
said ham , curiosity arises.

     How can Monsieur Horton OBtain another
specimen of same ??

     Marcella avers that Mrs H/ COOKed the ham,
I AM
as the wops say , in forse ,
                    as to whether sd HAM
was already cooked on arrival /

               this is a mere trivial
detail or not as the case may be/
     /   )

     it does matter whether those not in
possession of suitable machenery may attempt
to DEAL with the hind quarter of porker /

There is NO doubt that the Washington OUTLET
can be widened.

               enquiringly yrs

4 devotees ready to
issue proclamations
declHAMations.

Dear H.M.

iTEM, the 3 boxes stüffing, to great surprise of dogana
    who were looking for gramophone records etc.

the CElestial rump placed in jeopardy by difference of
calorificity of tiroleąn WOOD fire ,

                           first attempt appeared half raw/

secong fytte , i,e, 3 , no FOUR ,hours of boiling , and the
texture arrived at etc,
                    with flavour, believe it or knot
conserved.

              as the desert rat said : $80,000's worth
                                                OF

                  experience.

The haggis for Bobbie Burrns bicentennial yielded to local treatment.

Gratitude to ham-sender. Further experiments in process.

Is Zabaglione   current in Richmond ? or return receipts

Brillat Savarin etc/

rather weakened from flu , so please excuse delays and paucity
of utterance.

"ecd/ Am/ "eritage

              10 Feb

I dont spose
poEm ? by E Z P. you know any periodical in the U.S. that wants a
Or that wants serious articles by Swabey etc. else ?
                    ၈) anyone
                  benedictions. Am at any rate able to
sit up and read Uncle Remus.

                  yours ever

26 Dec. 58

Dear Meacham

        Joyous Xmas, etc. The sacred ham has not yet   arruv.

Mail seems fairly constant for letters but packets are NOTHER
matter. arrests usually made too late to recover the property.

Of course it may still get here, and in any case thanks. We did o.k
on a turkey ,
            which peregrine fowl the Tirolese genius in the kitch
refused to touch ,
                 but did judge roasting time/   100 %
                                    But no stuffing.

It occurs to me that Mrs Meacham may have some   specially DEElight
recipe for what OUGHT to be inside the next one.

alZo that she might send DIrections re/ construction of Sally Lunn.

there is no need to lose the remaining years of one's pilgrimage
because of ignorance of essentials.

Best to the lot of YOU for 59.

ANY news of villas in the SUN and south of europe wd/ be welcome
Naturally the so called American Academy in Rome, OUGHT to give me
a roof.

        believe now fallen into claws for Mr Cowslip's insteroot.

also Mrs Raiola tried to get space in a villa donated to
the Virgilian Society / but they ousted her .
                                    No news that the So.

DOES anything useful /

new evaluation of celebrities who have either accepted
the brain-wash or collaborated in it , is WANTED.

ra Pound, the child, and his family

Ezra Pound at Saint Elizabeth's

Ezra Pound in 1920

Courtesy of *L'Herne*.

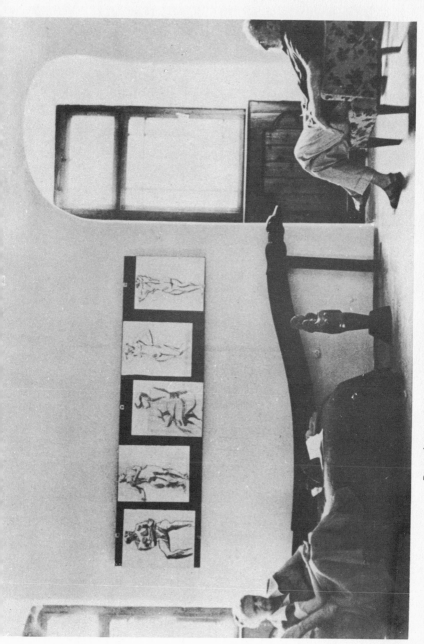

Dorothy and Ezra Pound in the Gaudier-Brzeska Flat.

Ezra Pound and Harry Meacham at Jamestown, May 1, 1958.

Photo by Dean W. Melville Jones of William & Mary College

23 November 1957

PERSONAL AND CONFIDENTIAL

Dear Mr. Meacham,

I thank you for your letter of 18 October. My reply has been delayed because I hoped for some further information before telling you about my views on the question you raise.

I am indeed most interested in securing Mr. Pound's release. I have done what I could in order to further a possible solution. However, I am insufficiently informed about the results of my efforts so far to say anything about them.

What I have tried to do has been linked up with efforts of others concerning which I may perhaps refer you to Professor Archibald MacLeish at Harvard with whom you undoubtedly have been in touch already.

I agree with you that any publicity at this time would be ruinous and our exchange of views will be kept on a strictly confidential basis by me as I trust also by you.

I would appreciate any information you might care to give me about further developments. If you see any point on which I might be helpful, I am sure that you will inform me.

Sincerely

Dag Hammarskjöld

Mr. Harry M. Meacham
P.O. Box 1376
Richmond, Va.

29 0 c   57

Dear H.M.

        I have told Giovannini   I trust your sincerity.

ₕave you heard from MacLiesh ? and are you able to get ANY id

what he thinks about histɒry , or whether he has ANY idea of

my position re/ balance of power in Eᵾrope or anything   else

Or whether he thinks you can collaborate with him ?

                                                  yrz   E.P.

ᵓandburg was being mildly   regretful on TV Sunday

Courtesy of the *Richmond News Leader*.

3514 Brothers Place

Dear Meacham

              Thanks for yrs~ of the whateverth and the enclosures ,

Let us CORRECT at once Mr Fridell's unintentional   attribution of
false modesty , to you and their correspondent,

I did NOT say Yeats was a better writer than I am , or Was

Fridddell is an excellent reporter with an almost perfect verbal
memory but he missed the connecting words,

I was quoting Ford Madox Ford , who said, i.e FORD said : " Of course
Yeats is a much greater WRITER POET than I am , BUT he is a gargoyle, "

Get the EXACT shade, Ford did not say BETTER poet , he most certainly
and ABsolutely did NOT think Yeats a better WRITER

                                        His words were what he mean

iie. a GREATER   POET
                         adjective greater , noun POET.

***
More serious is the statement that I broadcast FOR the Wartime Fascist
government,
                                                    of wangling etc
            It took me , I think it was TWO years , insistence to GET
            HOLD of their microphone, and repeated time and TIME
again :

     " This is what Brooks Adams said in 1903   or this is what B, Adams
PRINTED in 1897

                 CAN this be Axis Propaganda ??   "

***
Coming to future felicities , WHAT could Eliot do for your
poetry society that I can't ?

Marcella is coming to Richmond on or about the 17 th inst,

she could import and export D, P, and myself , saving you making two
trip , to Washington and back,
                                             publicly
         Would that be too soon to rake in the price of steamship
tickets , by answering the questions in yr~ letter, TO the
assembled egg-heads and leaders of the Southern poetic renaissance,
                I haven t
At any rate havent time to answer 'em in this letter, which
will be posted tomorrow and possibly reach you by Tuesday,

best TO no ladies gawd bless 'um

(left margin, rotated): she had early classes Monday, so shd~ want to leave on Sunday early Marcella od~ bring us on Friday 16 or sat 14 18 th at latest

Dorothy Pound during the 1930

Harry M. Meacham

Courtesy of *L'Herne*.

conducive to any public stir. Too many in and out of government shared Robert Frost's sentiments, which were that Pound was where he belonged.

When Hemingway spoke out at Stockholm, those who had been waiting for improved conditions took heart. The attitude of the United States government had not softened, but men of letters all over the world began to ask embarrassing questions. As MacLeish continued to probe for a soft spot in the wall of hostility, he realized that the "germane ideas" Pound was writing about and discussing with all and sundry multiplied his difficulties. There were too many ideas in action; all, or almost all, controversial. Eliot made the same discovery and wrote MacLeish, deploring the fact that Pound wrote letters to Secretary of State Herter and others who had neither met the poet nor heard from him before. "It is very difficult," he wrote, "to persuade people that Ezra is neither sane nor insane, that he has already served a sufficient term of imprisonment to cover his misdemeanors, and that he would be no greater danger to society out of St. Elizabeths than in it. The only persons Ezra's freedom could possibly injure are himself and his immediate kin."

Since the situation was critical, Mr. MacLeish reluctantly wrote Pound a short, friendly letter, no doubt hoping to convince him that further propagandizing for his principles from a ward in an insane asylum was both futile and damaging. He also suggested that Pound failed to understand the weight of the indictment against him. "Is it not a fact," he asked, "that there is no one in the United States (except yourself) who understands that your broadcasts from Italy were a duty to the American public, but that you did not then understand they would be construed as treason according to the law of the country from which you claimed citizenship? If you want complete exoneration and a conversion of the U. S. official mind to the views you then expressed, the practical view is you are asking the impossible to expect any American government to condemn their officials for their resistance to your views. . . ."

And so MacLeish increased the tempo of his activities in Pound's behalf. In July 1956 he asked Senator Fulbright if he would look into the situation. The Senator said he would have an assistant check into it. Meanwhile, Eliot visited Pound during his annual visit to the United States in 1956. He reported to MacLeish that he had wanted to see Dr. Overholser but was unable to arrange a meeting and commissioned a trusted friend to talk to the psychiatrist. This friend quoted Dr. Overholser as saying Pound was not insane at that time and could leave the hospital at once. In December the Superintendent wrote MacLeish: "Your understanding is quite correct. I think it is high time that charges against Pound should be dropped, but I think that his release from the Hospital at this time would muddy the waters to an undesirable extent."

Dr. Overholser's role in the Pound drama is an interesting one. As one of the four psychiatrists appointed by the court to examine Pound, later certifying that he was mentally unfit to stand trial, and, as Superintendent of St. Elizabeths the poet's legal custodian, it is only natural to think of him as a government witness, and a hostile one. But nothing could be further from the truth. He was Pound's friend, a scholarly man who read the poet's writings as they appeared; a gentle man who showed Pound every consideration consistent with his responsibilities as head of the government's largest mental institution. There is no question but that he had the best interests of his government and his distinguished patient in mind and that he consulted with Mr. MacLeish in working out a plan to get the poet out of the hospital.

Dr. Winfred Overholser (1892-1964) was for more than thirty years one of this country's leading psychiatrists. Formerly Commissioner of Mental Diseases for the state of Massachusetts, he was appointed head of St. Elizabeths by President Franklin D. Roosevelt in 1937; he retired in 1962. He served as President of the American Psychiatric Association, as Professor of Psychiatry at George Washington University School of Medicine, and was the recipient in 1952 of the Issac Ray Award of The American Psychiatric Association. He also guided the pioneering use of tranquilizers and other new therapeutic agents and techniques for the treatment of the mentally ill.

Among the many ironic twists in the tragic and bizarre plight of the poet are the letters the patient wrote the doctor, for they are, in fact, the notes of one man of letters to another. On July 25, 1950 he wrote the Superintendent: "W.O. perfectly welcome to see me re book [*Patria Mia*] but ought to have better way (i.e., more contemporary) of spending his time." There must have been many such communications, for in 1957 he wrote a long letter to Dr. Overholser from which I have excerpted the following: "I think you saw Jap/ bilingual Mauberley . . . as per this a. m. 3245 copies Lustra put into Polish by Niemojowski, in cellar at Warsaw awaiting Gomulka pleasure . . . Univs. of Calif. and Cambridge Eng/ vast INDEX to Cantos, '7,500 items, 17,000 references' some idiotic, but very good job on the greek by a bloke named Peachey . . . Did I forget to give you a Universidad Mexico review re/ Jimeniz. Best for '58 to you and Mrs. Overholser proles, nepotes and clausi . . . Meacham has rolled up Van W. [yck] Brooks also, or enrolled, or whatever the verb is. E.P."

On August 1, 1959 Pound wrote this note from Rapallo, Italy:

DEAR W. O.

I don't know whether you will ever get credit for making possible the Confucian Anthology and two vols. of Cantos.

At any rate my thanks. and thanks to King.[29] Whatever became of him. I thought he stuck his neck out possibly the furthest.

Yrs

E. P.

Dag Hammarskjöld, Secretary-General of the United Nations, outstanding scholar and a member of the Swedish Academy, greatly admired Pound's writings, and there are unconfirmed reports that he nominated the poet for the Nobel Prize in Literature. He had also been getting in a few blows for liberty. In November 1956, he wrote Mr. MacLeish he had read his *New York Times* review of *Section: Rock Drill* with "high appreciation," adding, "You may know that—with the discretion imposed upon me by my office—I have been doing what I can in order to straighten out Pound's situation." He pointed out (significantly, I think) that his colleagues in the Swedish Academy authorized him to do this.

As the drive gathered momentum, Hammarskjöld wrote Francis Wilcox, Assistant Secretary of State, expressing his hope and the hope of his colleagues in the Academy that a way would be found to drop the charges against the poet. There had also been some correspondence between MacLeish and Dr. Milton Eisenhower, brother of the General and President of Johns Hopkins University, concerning the Pound case. The two were and are, old friends. In the last exchange relating to the poet, Dr. Eisenhower, without indicating that he would help in any way (and there is no record that he did) said if Pound were released he would expect the charges to be pressed, adding that though he might be a good poet, this was immaterial.

MacLeish's reply spells out the position of poets and men of letters throughout the world with such clarity that it is a document of constellatory importance, to borrow a phrase from Charles Lamb:

WIDENER W CAMBRIDGE 38
January 11 1957

DEAR MILTON:

I am still hard at work on the Ezra Pound matter about which I wrote you some time ago. After careful consultation with authorities at St. Elizabeths, including Dr. Overholser, I can say with confidence that it is the opinion of the responsible doctors that Pound is not now fit to stand trial and never will be. Under these circumstances the perpetuation of the legal charges against him seems to be irrelevant, not to put a stronger word to it. Robert Frost, T. S. Eliot and Ernest Hemingway are therefore writing the Attorney General suggesting that in view of his eleven years incarceration the nol prossing of the charges against Pound would be in order, not only in the interests of common humanity, but in the interest of the good name of the United States.

I know that you dissent from my view on the latter point. You wrote me, as you may recall, that it makes no difference whatever that Pound is a poet. In terms of logic this may be true but in terms of history and of civilization it is not. As you know better than I, nations are judged in the perspective of history by the way they treat their poets, philosophers, artists and teachers.

The reason for this present letter relates to this fact. I have the very best reason to believe that Pound is shortly to be awarded the Nobel Prize in Literature. I can think of nothing which would make this country look more ridiculous than to hold in an insane asylum, under criminal indictment, a recipient of the Nobel Prize in literature. Everything our most virulent critics say about us would be justified by that single dramatic fact. If our action in so holding him could be justified in common sense we could perhaps shrug it off, but since in view of the medical testimony it cannot be justified we would look very silly indeed.

I trouble you with all this, not to try to convert you to my view but because I care deeply, as you do, about the repute of this republic, and because you are in a position to do something about it. I need not add that what I have told you about the Nobel Prize situation should be treated as confidential, except in so far as its repetition in confidence might help to bring about the desired action. By the desired action I refer solely, at this time, to the quashing of the charges, then remitting the whole problem of Pound's future to the medics who ought to dispose of it.

Forgive me for troubling you with all this again.

Affectionately

ARCHIE

While it cannot be confirmed, it is reliably reported that Pound had been nominated for the Nobel prize, and since he had a powerful advocate in Dag Hammarskjöld, Mr. MacLeish had every reason to believe Pound would get it.[30] The poet was also nominated for the Gold Medal of the American Academy of Arts and Letters, but this was withdrawn. The ruckus over the Bollingen[31] had made cowards of us all.

The letter to the then Attorney General Herbert Brownell, printed below, was drafted by MacLeish, then sent to Eliot in London, Hemingway in Cuba, and Frost in Vermont. Eliot and Hemingway suggested minor changes. Mr. Eliot felt his name should not be first, since he was an English citizen. MacLeish had first suggested that Carl Sandburg should also sign, but he changed his mind. Eliot approved of this, since he felt Sandburg's name would not help. MacLeish then arranged to have the final draft written on the letterhead of the American Academy of Arts and Letters.[32]

January 14, 1957

The Attorney General of the United States,
Washington
D. C.

DEAR SIR,

We are writing to you about Ezra Pound who has been confined in St. Elizabeths Hospital in Washington for eleven years under indictment for treason.

Our interest in this matter is founded in part on our concern for Mr. Pound who is one of the most distinguished American writers of his generation, and in part on our concern for the country of our birth. As writers ourselves we cannot but be aware of the effect on writers and lovers of literature throughout the world of Pound's continued incarceration at a time when certain Nazis tried and convicted of the most heinous crimes, have been released and in many cases rehabilitated.

It is our understanding, based on inquiries directed to the medical personnel at St. Elizabeths Hospital, that Pound is now unfit for trial and, in the opinion of the doctors treating him, will continue to be unfit for trial. This opinion, we believe, has already been communicated to the Department of Justice. Under these circumstances the perpetuation of the charges against him seems to us unfortunate and, indeed, indefensible. It provides occasion for criticism of American justice not only at home but abroad and it seems to us, in and of itself, unworthy of the traditions of the Republic. Concerned, as we must be, with the judgments of posterity on this unhappy affair, we cannot but regret the failure of the Department thus far to take steps to nol pros the indictment and remit the case to the medical authorities for disposition on medical grounds.

May we add that this is a personal letter to you and that we have no intention at this time of making a public statement on this matter.

Could we be of service to you, a letter addressed to us in care of the American Academy of Arts and Letters at 633 West 155th Street, New York City will have our immediate attention.

Faithfully yours,

ROBERT FROST
T. S. ELIOT
ERNEST HEMINGWAY

January 14, 1957

As the movement to free Pound gained force, MacLeish played his highest trump, Robert Frost. As Professor Lawrance Thompson has pointed out, "MacLeish conducted his backstage manipulations of RF with exceptional tact." The poet-diplomat had held high office in the Roosevelt Administration, but he had no influence with the Republicans, so he realized he must call in other literary giants whose names would carry weight with the Eisenhower Administration. Frost was the logical choice for the center of the stage as the climax of the drama approached. Not only was he our most famous poet, but the mask, the persona he had created, of a simple, chicken-raising farmer who had always been close to the soil, had made him America's most beloved writer.

Shortly after the Frost-Hemingway-Eliot letter reached the Attorney General, Hemingway wrote MacLeish that his lawyer had informed him the Executive Assistant Attorney General, Harold H. Early, desired to speak with the persons requesting the release of Ezra Pound, if any action was to be taken on the matter. All during Pound's incarceration Hemingway kept in touch with the situation, sometimes directly, but usually through MacLeish. As affairs took a more favorable turn he said he hoped Pound's hunting license would be restricted so that he would not write or indulge in politics; otherwise his enemies would get him to say "fool" things, and a certain type of journalist would provoke him into playing the role of anti-Semite, racist, and mad poet.

On July 22, 1957 MacLeish wrote Pound that he and Frost had visited "the boys at the Department of Justice last Friday." "For the immediate future," he continued, "and so long as the Kasper mess is boiling and stewing the Department will not move. . . . No commitments or near commitments were made. But the door wasn't closed and we were left with the impression that once the Kasper stink had blown over they would be willing to consider proposals."

The publicity linking Pound's name with Kasper's was a serious setback. In discussing the Pound case with me on April 13, 1967, former Attorney General William P. Rogers said that from the first he was sympathetic toward Pound, one of our great poets, and that he was also aware of growing world opinion that the poet should be released. He said he felt it was important to free Pound as soon as it was safe to do so. The machinery had been set in motion, he said, but the "Kasper mess" had brought everything to a standstill.

Mr. Rogers reminded me that the situation during Mr. Brownell's term of office had been critical, with troops in Little Rock and riots and dynamiting spearheaded by John Kasper delaying integration and in some instances keeping children out of school. I inferred that the Department of Justice believed Pound to be somehow connected with this violence, at least to the extent that he was advising Kasper, for Mr. Rogers said the Department felt that if he were released Pound might join Kasper in the South and people would be killed.

The former Attorney General said that although he could not recall details surrounding the visits of Robert Frost, he did remember seeing him twice, once, he thought, at the White House. When asked about Frost's influence on his decision to hold the hearing on April 18, 1958, he said he would have acted when he did no matter who had called on him. "I told Mr. Frost what I would have told anyone," he said. He emphasized that he was waiting for the civil rights crisis to pass, and neither Robert Frost nor anyone else persuaded him to do what he did, when he did it. He said he gathered from Frost that Pound had agreed to leave the country, and this was a factor in his decision.

When the definitive account of these events is written, I am convinced that it will absolve Pound from any connection with Kasper beyond their literary collaboration. In one of his letters to me Giovannini quotes Louis Zukofsky, one of the outstanding poets of the twentieth century, and a Jew, "E. P. is no more responsible for Kasper's actions than Aristotle for the Hollywood production of Alexander the

Great." I believe that literary historians will condemn the United States government for holding Pound for over thirteen years without a trial. Believing this, I can still understand why the Department of Justice declined to take any action while Kasper was in the newspaper headlines. As for Mr. Rogers' role, it is well to remember that five months and ten days after he became Attorney General of the United States, Ezra Pound was a free man.

It was now time for Robert Frost to occupy the stage, alone. But just as he had been silent during all the past years when Pound was at St. Elizabeths, he was now reluctant when the situation demanded action. On February 28, 1957 Attorney General Herbert Brownell acknowledged receipt of the Frost-Eliot-Hemingway letter in a note to Frost, and said he had asked that a review of the matter be made. Frost did not answer this letter, so MacLeish wrote Mrs. Kathleen Morrison[33] suggesting that she urge the poet to write to the Attorney General so that MacLeish could arrange an appointment. On June 24, Frost wrote the following letter to Mac-Leish:[34]

DEAR ARCHIE

My purpose holds to help you get Ezra loose though I won't say my misgivings in the whole matter haven't been increased by my talks with Eliot lately, who knows more about Ezra than anybody else and what we can hope to do for his salvation. I should hate to see Ezra die ignominiously in that wretched place where he is for a crime which if proven couldn't have kept him all these years in prison. So you go ahead and make an appointment with the Department of Justice. I suppose we might be prepared to answer for Ezra's relative sanity and ability to get himself taken care of out in the world. Neither you nor I would want to take him into our family or even into our neighborhood. I shall be acting largely on your judgment. I can't bear that anyone's fate should hang too much on mine.

I am tied up here for the moment. I could be in Washington for any time on Wednesday July 17 or Friday the 19th after three o'clock or Saturday. But I should have thought that this time of year wouldn't find people in Washington and the affair might better wait until the Fall.

So much for business—bad business. We mustn't forget the good relations we have promised to have with each other this summer.

Ever yours—on either side of the Atlantic

Frost's "talks with Eliot" took place in London in May. MacLeish, who was staying at the same hotel, again urged Frost to call on William Rogers in Washington. MacLeish replied to this letter at once. Still writing the script and prompting the actors, he said:

Bless you . . . I have asked Miss Geffen at the Academy to write the Deputy Attorney General asking whether July 19 (late in the PM) or the 20th would do. Of course I would go along if you want me. I have also written Ernest[35] asking him to send you a full statement of his views and I shall ask Tom[36] to do the same so that you will go fully armed. Maybe it would be easier if their letters came to me so that I could turn the whole file over to you.

More when I know more. It was good to see you in London.

Yours aye

ARCHIE

Then, as if by magic, everything fell into place. Richard Rovere wrote a sympathetic article for the September 1957 issue of *Esquire*, urging Pound's release, and this prompted letters to the editor from many famous writers, including Marianne Moore. Then Congressman Burdick introduced the Seiber report to which was attached a statement, and a strong one, from Dr. Giovannini. Coming almost on the heels of each other were the Frost-Eliot-Hemingway letter, the visits of MacLeish and Frost to the Department of Justice, a letter from MacLeish to Secretary of State Christian Herter urging him to see Dr. Overholser, followed by a note from Secretary Herter to Dr. Overholser suggesting that he drop in some day "to discuss this difficult individual Ezra Pound."

Then it was 1958, and freedom was three months away. On January 2, Attorney General Rogers, who had succeeded Herbert Brownell on November 8, 1957, wrote MacLeish: "I think the best thing to do is to discuss the matter with you when you are next in Washington. I am not sure whether it can be worked out or not, *but I am certainly inclined in that direction,* if it can be worked out from a legal standpoint . . ." (my italics). Then Rogers sent up a trial balloon at a New York press conference. The *New York Times* of April 2 said: "Attorney General William P. Rogers disclosed . . . that Ezra Pound may escape trial and be allowed to go to Italy." On the whole, public response was favorable, and freedom was a step closer. Having prepared press and public, it was then necessary to set the stage with the utmost care, and this was done with consummate skill. Frost went to the White House to see his old friend Sherman Adams, who was considered by many to be the most powerful figure in Washington, next to President Eisenhower. Governor Adams arranged for another meeting between Rogers and Frost, a meeting so brief it might have been rehearsed. Frost said to Rogers: "I've dropped in to see what your mood is in regard to Ezra Pound." Rogers said to Frost: "Our mood is your mood, Mr. Frost."

It was then arranged for Frost to see William [Will] Shafroth, Deputy Director of the Administrative Office of the United States Courts, to arrange for an attorney to represent Pound. He recommended Thurman Arnold of the law firm of Arnold, Fortes and Porter (Julien Cornell, an able lawyer and still Pound's attorney of record, was somehow lost in the shuffle), and it proved to be a fortunate choice. As Mr. Arnold points out in his book, *Fair Fights and Foul,* there was a procedural difficulty, since Frost approached him without consulting Mrs. Pound. However, Dorothy called on him the day after Frost saw him and asked Arnold to take the case. He represented Mr. Pound but would not accept a fee.

When Ezra was visiting me in Richmond, he mentioned casually that he understood details of the final hearing were worked out at a Cabinet meeting. The case did reach the White House, but the Cabinet meeting would have involved the President, so I asked Governor Adams about it. In his reply he did not mention Mr. Eisenhower but confirmed that he had arranged the Frost-Rogers meeting, adding, "and what I did thereafter was at Frost's instigation." My question still unanswered, I wrote President Eisenhower and asked, "Did you personally give the nod to the Department of Justice that resulted in a pre-hearing agreement to dismiss the indictments against Ezra Pound?" On August 20, 1963 his son, Lieutenant Colonel John Eisenhower, answered, in part, "I have checked with those who should know and found no evidence of any White House participation in the action on the part of the Department of Justice." He went on to say, "I am sure you have seen the reference to Pound's release in Governor Adams' book. The implication there is strong that Robert Frost was successful in negotiating this release by himself."

As it turned out, there was no pre-trial "deal," although there were some discussions. Mr. Arnold asked the Department of Justice what position it would take if he filed a motion to dismiss. "The Department said it was not in a position to give me any information."[37] Of his approach to the case, he wrote, "As I have indicated, the only way to liberate Pound without offending the logic of the law was to dismiss the indictment. This the Attorney General declined to do for understandable reasons. To take affirmative action liberating a man who had broadcast against the United States in time of war, and who in addition was a notorious anti-Semite, would have put the Department of Justice under sharp attack. But I had gathered from Frost that while the Attorney

General would not affirmatively dismiss the indictment, he would not oppose a motion to dismiss if I made it." And that is how it was finally done.

The end came as an anticlimax. On April 18, 1958, the case of the *United States* v. *Ezra Pound*, defendant, was heard in the United States District Court for the District of Columbia. Those who had worked to bring this about and who were not privy to the pre-trial conferences, feared the government attorney might insist that since Pound was adjudged insane, he might be required to remain in this country subject to another hearing if and when psychiatrists found he could stand trial.

It seemed the government wanted Pound out of the way, and out of the country, as soon as possible, so our fears were groundless. Mr. Oliver Gasch, U. S. Attorney, said he had studied the affidavit of Dr. Overholser (submitted in support of Mr. Arnold's motion) and was satisfied of the incompetency of the defendant to stand trial. He added that it would be virtually impossible to produce evidence of Mr. Pound's sanity during the war years in Italy, and he consented to Mr. Arnold's motion. The hearing lasted but a few minutes.

I thought Mr. MacLeish was out of the country, so I sent him a clipping about the hearing, adding as a footnote that I knew and Ezra knew that he, more than anyone else, was responsible for the result of the hearing. I said I felt sure Ezra would write him about it. Mr. MacLeish in his reply, printed below, is right about Pound's scolding, but this was his way with his friends and it was a certain sign of affection. Behind the mask, the brusqueness, there was a warm-hearted, generous man. There was about Ezra what poet Hayden Carruth said about his art, "a splendid light, a luminosity." In his critique, "Ezra Pound and the Great Style" in *The Saturday Review*, April 9, 1966, Mr. Carruth, in examining Pound's vision of the Good, says, "Hotheaded, impulsive, irascible, yes; but you may search as you will through his poems, essays, prose fragments and personal correspondence (as far as it is available) and you will not find a scrap of a personal motive—no private ambition, not even a general desire for power, since he has continually thrown away all the power he actually had." No ordinary man, involved deeply in difficulties of his own making, could have held the friendship of such of the great as MacLeish, Hemingway, Eliot, Marianne Moore, Cummings, William Carlos Williams, Dag Hammarskjöld, and a score of others.

I do not know anything about the relationship between MacLeish and Pound over the years except what is in the letters and what I read between the lines. I suspect much good-natured banter passed between them, and there is certainly a touch of wry humor in MacLeish's note. Pound never gave up trying to convert his old friend. "I ain't deespaired of savin' yr/ soul," he once wrote, "slowly perhaps and in fragments, but still . . ." Then, as an afterthought, scrawled in the corner, "as one drammertist to another." In another brief note he asked, "How do you spend your time of mind, anyhow?" and added, "Gawd bless and keep you in a waverin' world."

To return to Mr. MacLeish's reply to my letter containing an account of the final hearing:

UPHILL FARM, CONWAY, MASSACHUSETTS

May 7, 1958

DEAR MR. MEACHAM:

I am grateful for your note and its enclosure. But please don't trouble about my credit for the happy outcome. I have never expected or really wanted an expression of gratitude from Ezra. On the contrary I expected what I have gotten—weekly excoriations followed by silence. Actually I think you yourself deserve far more credit than you are likely, in your generous modesty, to admit.

With warm regards

ARCHIBALD MACLEISH

After a long look at the record and a careful study of files restricted until they were opened to me, I can truthfully say, without being either generous or modest, that I have received far more credit from Mr. MacLeish and Ezra Pound than I am entitled to.

PART THREE

EXCEPT FOR A FEW OLD FRIENDS and a few new ones he made during his long confinement, Pound was the forgotten man, but from the day the indictment for treason was dismissed until he sailed for Italy, the poet was news. Mrs. Pound had gone to Boston to escape reporters and was visiting her son Omar, and Ezra was virtually in seclusion.

On April 19, while he was still in the hospital having some dental work completed, I drove to Washington to see what I could do to help and to arrange for his visit to Richmond. We went first to a small semiprivate room on the ward where he was permitted to write—always with the door open. We made several trips to my car, loaded down with boxes, bags, manuscripts, books, and other memorabilia which we deposited in Mrs. Pound's dingy apartment on Nichols Avenue, S. E., about twenty blocks from St. Elizabeths. Pound gave me copies of several literary journals, which contained one or more cantos, as well as several photographs I admired; one, I prize highly, was a picture of the hieratic head of Pound by Gaudier-Brzeska.

There was much mail waiting for him, but he ignored everything but a book, which turned out to be a new, revised edition of *Pavannes and Divigations* (New Directions, 1958). He admired the binding and smiled at Rex Lampman's "epitaph" on the flyleaf ("Here he lies, The Idaho Kid,/ The only time he ever did.") Then as we sat in the car he leafed hurriedly through the volume until he found Ernest Hemingway's contribution:

NEOTHOMIST POEM

The Lord is my Shepherd,
I shall not want
Him for long.

This seemed to please him enormously, and he read it

131

several times, aloud. Then we headed for a Chinese restaurant
nearby. I wanted to take him to Washington's best, but his
mind was made up. Whether he was drawn by the Chinese,
the food, or the quiet, was his own business. At any rate, he
consumed his order of chicken chow mein and mine also, and
he talked, talked, talked.

There was some question about if and when the poet would
get his passport. I was uneasy about this and along with other
friends urged Pound not to grant an interview until this
delicate matter was settled. I am sure Pound was the poorest
public relations man in all literature. Every time he opened
his mouth he put his foot in it, and this situation was no
exception. He called on Congressman Burdick, who had
helped him, and he spoke bluntly to reporters there. Also,
in a brief encounter at the courthouse a newspaperman asked
him about Frost's efforts in his behalf. The poet replied, "He
ain't been in much of a hurry."

As Pound drank cup after cup of tea I reminded him of
this statement. Then I read aloud an editorial in which it
was stated that after forty years Frost had repaid Pound for
his help in London. Pound smiled and said, "Frost's debt was
paid when he published *North of Boston*."

I thought that statement was magnificent; and I thought,
also, that it might be a clue to his character. Pound felt no
one should be obligated to him for anything he had done for
them, and he, in turn, never felt he was under obligation for
any services, of whatever magnitude. The only acknowledg-
ment he made of my efforts in his behalf—that is, prior to his
last two letters to me—was his inscription in my copy of the
Translations of Ezra Pound, which I did not discover for
some months: "To H. M. Meacham, with tanks for his
subterranean activities."

While Pound was eating and I was drinking black coffee,
we were making plans for his forthcoming visit to my home
in Richmond. I asked him to grant an exclusive interview to

the *News-Leader*, since Kilpatrick was to meet with us, but he said he preferred not to do this under the circumstances. Then he drew an envelope from his inner pocket and wrote the following "interview," which I dutifully passed on to Mr. Kilpatrick. However, when we reached Richmond, Pound consented to the interview which turned out so well the brief note was not needed. Here, then, is the "interview," appearing for the first time, and still a Kilpatrick-*News-Leader* exclusive.

After repeating his statement about Frost's payment of his debt, he said, "E. P. on way to Richmond, wants to see some of the old south—and have his family see some. Effort worth it if a few more people were interested in the Va. Bill of Rights and Connecticut Charter. Exclusive to News Leader JJK. by their special correspondent."

(25)

25 April 58

DEAR MEACHAM

Oke?? I will be here waiting for you on Wednesday a.m. ap. ult.

Took the Günter Blöcker "Neuen Wirklickeiten" to Gilhoff yester, and he will review it at length desired by Va ¼ly. If the Va ¼ly wants it, which I shd/ think they would.

I don't know if their service is for Germany and North Europe,
                                                but doubt if they
cd/ get a better man than Gilhoff for regular "eye"
                                ready to do the notes of
whatever
length they want, on the few, and they are DAMN FEW books that ought to be noticed.

He cd/ also do the Goullart Forgotten Kingdom.

And as Goullart has two new books to appear, with Murray (London) the ¼ly wd/ be on the job waiting to get 'em before the incult s.o.b's know they are there.

Giovannini has just phoned that he will edit the Rosetti Agresti-Pound correspondence.

so we can discuss this with Miss Kohler, etc.

Please send me a copy of the N. Leader if they use my "exclusive."

benedictions

E. P.

address for Meacham and no one else

3514 Brothers Place, S. E.

Burdick is out of hospital, but not seeing anyone till next week, had word from him and have returned the greetings. This not for release.

Chicago Trib excellent. Some of the lies by wops wanting to get on the bandwagon are very amusing. Mebbe the N. Leader cd ironize on the state of wop press under dummy Xt slop.

(26)

26 Ap 1958

"Doan' yu think he chop an' change all the time,
stubborn az as mule, saH, stubborn as a MULE!"

end quote

H. M.

to apply that much of the noble passage to nobler things. I said Wednesday, and Wednesday I shall be deelighted.

Do not expect D. P. back from Boston by then, but suggest you accept also Fred Grab

just

back from China, India, etc. and struggling with state dept, for right to travel.

will probably have

stuff not send via A. P. etc. Unless you cable contrary ukase I will have F. G. on these premises, 3514 Brothers Pl. from 9 a.m. onwards

Yrz

E. P.

(27)

(4/28/58)

Monday

Dear H. M.

Sorry, cant run to more than my exclusive that I gave you.
plus foto, if you like.
But no interview at this time. At any rate not to be released
until I get my visa,

and all clear and am finally discharged
from hospital.

yrz

E. P.

hurrying to dental appointment.

On the morning of April 30 I presented myself at the
apartment of Mrs. Pound to pick up Ezra and Fred Grab
for the drive to Richmond. It would be difficult to find, and
impossible to describe, more dismal and depressing surroundings. The apartment was in the basement of an old frame
dwelling and was small, damp, and poorly ventilated. The
only light came from low-watt, unprotected bulbs suspended
from the ceiling, and it was crowded with the accumulations
of a lifetime. Dorothy had lived in the place for the last six
years of Pound's detention and had walked to the hospital
every day. Since Pound had been at St. Elizabeths she had
been his legal guardian, so her mornings were taken up with
correspondence and business matters in order to free her
afternoons to visit Ezra.

As we prepared to leave for Virginia it was apparent that
the poet was mentally and physically exhausted, so I put
him in the back seat, where he reclined during the two-and-a-
half-hour drive. And for once he had very little to say. We
stopped at a roadside restaurant near Fredericksburg for lunch.
He grumbled about the food, saying it was as bad as anything he had encountered at the hospital. We bought a

Washington paper and found a report of his visit with Congressman Burdick played up on the front page. However, there was no formal interview with Pound. The first interview since his release was to come within two hours.

We were late in leaving Washington and had lingered too long over lunch, so the party I had arranged at the Rotunda Club had waited for more than an hour beyond the appointed time. Present were Mrs. James Branch Cabell; James J. Kilpatrick; Guy Friddell, columnist and political writer for the *News-Leader*; Miss Charlotte Kohler, editor of the *Virginia Quarterly Review*; and William Gresham, who would succeed me as president of The Poetry Society of Virginia.

It was an unforgettable afternoon. The club occupies all of the north side of the Jefferson Hotel, an old and elegant hotel located in what was once the best residential area in Virginia. Nearby were the old homes of the Cabells, the Glasgows, the Valentines as well as the Richmond residence of General Robert E. Lee. When introductions had been completed and refreshments served (the poet declined the traditional bourbon and water but drank two glasses of sherry), Mrs. Cabell said that James, who was ill, "Sent the thanks he owes you for many happy hours." Pound was delighted and jumped up: "Can't we go hold his hand?" Back in the 1920's, as co-editor of *The Reviewer*, published in Richmond, she had printed Gertrude Stein's "Indian Boy" and "Van, or Twenty Years After" while other journals were ridiculing the experimentalist, so Mrs. Cabell and Pound got along famously, and he referred to her in his letters from Italy. Guy Friddell, now editor of the editorial page of the *Norfolk Virginian-Pilot*, wrote an excellent story on the gathering which was picked up by the Associated Press and sent around the world. When the poet referred to the "gorilla cage" at Pisa and observed, wryly, "Few men of letters have those opportunities," the guests were amused and touched.

I was to recall this statement later when Mrs. Pound, writing of the Disciplinary Training Center, said, "I don't know how one lives through such things."

James Kilpatrick, now a nationally syndicated columnist, wrote an article for *The National Review*, "A Conversation with Ezra Pound,"[1] which I think belongs in this book, and so it is reprinted in its entirety.

A Conversation with Ezra Pound

The poet who spent twelve years
in "St. Liz" proves to be
eccentric, often obscure, sane   JAMES JACKSON KILPATRICK
and sometimes acutely wise

On April 18, the Department of Justice dismissed a 13-year-old indictment against Ezra Pound, and a week later the authorities at St. Elizabeths Hospital in Washington placed this aging poet on an outpatient status. On the afternoon of April 30, Pound drove to Richmond in the company of Harry Meacham, president of the Virginia Poetry Society, and for a little more than two hours we talked together in the oddly chaste and dulcet surroundings of the Rotunda Club here.

This account of that causerie—surely it was nothing so formal as an interview—should be qualified at the outset: We did not talk serious politics. It is useless to talk serious politics with Ezra Pound. He is the last statesman of a lost cause—a cause lost a thousand years ago—and most of his enemies are dust. Talking with him, it is difficult to separate his live antagonists from the dead ones, the Rothschilds of 1750 from their counterparts two centuries later; and there is this problem for the ignoramus, meaning me, that when Pound touches a subject he does not so much touch it as embrace it. His mind is a river that holds ten thousand years of sand, but it deposits little sediment in washing over the untutored listener. Coleridge once remarked that the best poetry is that which is only generally, and not precisely, understood; and what I am groping to say is that I do not understand Pound even generally. Acknowledging that he is "anti-Semitic," I venture the positive assertion that Pound's anti-Semitism never will inspire the faintest urge in anyone to put a torch to a synagogue; a less effective rabble-rouser could not be conceived. The rabble would not understand a word that he says.

I offer this impression also: if words have any meaning left, Ezra Pound surely is no lunatic; and if it is true, as Dr. Overholser says, that Pound's condition has not changed since he entered St. Elizabeths in 1946, then Pound was no lunatic then. Obscure, yes; eccentric, yes; full of apparent confusion, yes. But crazy, no.

He was twenty minutes late arriving for our appointment. The party had left Washington on time, but had stopped midway for a sandwich, and Pound's dentures had proved inadequate for Howard Johnson's corned beef. They had taken their time to inspect the countryside—Rip Van Winkle absorbed in the neon mountains of Route One—and Pound had found the traffic incredible.

"All the time I was in the bughouse," he remarked, "I kept saying there were 160 million units outside, but I didn't realize what the poor devils were up against."

He shakes hands with the hard grip and strong forearm of a man who has played much tennis, and he dominates a room as if his armchair were down-stage center. He wore an open-necked shirt of a particularly god-awful magenta, tails out, and a pair of outsized slacks with the cuffs rolled up. A black coat, flung clockwise over his shoulders, completed the costume. If the description sounds theatrical, it is intended to suggest that there is in Pound a good deal of the actor, a good deal, indeed, of the ham. His bearded face, mobile, is the bust of some morning-after Bacchus; but it is seldom in repose. He sits on the lower part of his spine, head supported on the backrest of the chair, eyes closed; his restless hands are forever searching for glasses, or plucking pencil and notebook from a breast pocket, or shaping ideas in the air. Now and again, he bolts from his chair like some Poseidon from the deep, and his good eye—his right eye—is suddenly shrewd and alive.

On Education

Pound opened the conversation by bringing me a message from a Mrs. Lane in Arlington (*National Review*, April 19) and by commenting sociably upon his pleasure in visiting the South. I inquired, in the same agreeable vein, what he wanted most to do now that his full release was in prospect. The question was intended as no more than an ice-breaker, but Pound took it seriously. He said, leaping up, that God knew there was enough to be done right here. "What about some constitutional government in this country?" "What about this filth that passes for education?"

He began to talk generally of education. From everything he could read (he hated to read, reading was abominable, nothing but pulp came from publishers anyhow; Bowen's *Coke* was a masterpiece; it was a travesty upon the name of education that he was seventy years old, and in his second kindergarten, before he discovered Coke's *Institutes*)—from everything he could read (he read nothing any more, none of the contemporary works amount to a damn?)—from everything he could read, the schools are full of bilge. College freshmen should be required to know two languages, at least one of them inflected, and should be obliged to take analytics; and they should study U.S. history, not by way of Tocqueville and "Sandbag," or Toynbee (Toynbee is flapdoodle), but rather by way of Adams, Van Buren and Benton. It is nonsense for illiterates to be teaching the future when they know nothing of the past.

I single out these observations from a torrent of conversation, much as one plucks a recognizable rooftop from a flood. Pound no sooner launches one thought than he embarks upon another, and I summarize his critique of today's classrooms as one collects miscellaneous fishes after some volcanic churning on the ocean floor. He was thus, in his own fashion, treating current poetry by commenting upon the Italian foreign office in the days of Mussolini, when he sensed that he had lost me altogether.

"I really do have an orderly mind," he said abruptly. And then in a penetrating sentence: "I only want to make certain my interlocutors know the beginnings." Then he was off again, into the causes of war, the suppression of historic truth (of one historian, banished to obscurity by the educationists, Pound had an epitaph: "Poor Fellow, he committed accuracy"),[2] the corruption of the Federal Reserve Board, the usury rates of Byzantium, the reasons why he had not translated a particular Chinese writer, the enduring characteristics of the Manchu Dynasty, the old days in London with Ford Madox Ford. It was wonderful to eat something hot; he had forgotten what it meant for food to be hot.

At Rapallo there are surf rafts, and one floats on a blue sea. Had he mentioned that Hemingway once sent him a shark's jaw, the grave of the unknown sailor?

Again the pause, the bright and searching eye. "I don't have a one-track mind," he apologized. He slumped back; he apologized for slumping: "I cannot hold my head up for long; I have to rest it on something; I offered to be tried *in camera,* lying on a couch, but their reverences thought not; no wonder my head hurts, all of Europe fell on it; when I talk it is like an explosion in an art museum, you have to hunt around for the pieces."

Our small group included Miss Charlotte Kohler, editor of the *Virginia Quarterly Review.* Pound had corresponded with her over a long period of time (his code writing reduces the journal to the Va. ¼-ly Rev.), and she had brought galley proofs of several additional poems in the Pisan Cantos that will appear in the *Review* this summer. Pound observed benignly that all literary quarterlies are mutton, dead from the neck up, and inquired what Miss Kohler might do to improve the situation. She is a brilliant and attractive woman, with a tough, resilient mind, and after a brief defense tossed the question back at him.

On Ideas

He said, responding to one of her comments, that variety alone is not enough. There has to be some excitement, and the only way to get that is to put a couple of good minds in range of each other, and let them go to eye-gouging. This took him back to Wyndham Lewis, and to Ford again, and to Yeats. He was asked how he happened to encourage Yeats, twenty years his senior, when he was in a position to do so in England and Ireland forty years ago. He said he thought Yeats was the greatest poet in the world, discovered he wasn't; Yeats is a gargoyle; Eliot is spoiled by the company he keeps. "Dammit, you've got to examine ideas one at a time; I don't care whether the idea you put in your review comes from a Bolshevik, a Fascist, or a bloody pinko, his idea ought to be examined by itself."

Miss Kohler commented that Pound's Cantos obviously are still incomplete at the point marked by the manuscript he had sent her, and this led Pound into an extended comparative analysis of *La Divina Commedia.* I am sophomore-ignorant of Dante, and the conversation passed clean over my head; but it was evident that Pound was here speaking with easy sureness and a confident grasp of the complexities of both his work and Dante's. His own parallel characters have now passed through Hell and Purgatory and are somewhere in Paradise. When you paint on a big canvas, he said, gesturing largely, you have to start colors down here, gesturing small, but it all ties in, it all ties in.

As for explicating some of his more obscure passages, he had once spent four pages explaining a two-line poem (and that reminded him of a two-line poem by Hemingway; what is the one big reason for the survival of the Catholic Church? Versatility), and damned if he would add to that. He was asked to explain his work often enough. When the word came that he was coming out of St. Liz, an invitation arrived from some group, he could not remember the name, devoted to pondering the aesthetics of aesthetics, and to making higher criticism of the higher criticism. What an omelet their meeting must be! Yolks of the largest and freshest eggheads only. Winchell was not all bad. Winchell had raised hell when Elliott Roosevelt bumped a civilian off the plane so his damned dog could have a ride. And that reminded him of the story of little Abraham who had to write a sentence using the words "once" and "twice." He wrote: "While I was sleeping in my bed last night, I was bit by a Wuntz, twice." What the Fed is doing to the monetary supply is not new. Once, twice. And back to Byzantium.

On Writing and Reading

It was past five o'clock by this time, and Pound was tiring. As we rose to go, someone, still searching for a brief and useful quote, asked Pound what he would advise young writers to do. Surprisingly, he was terse and to the point: "Get a good dictionary and learn the meaning of words." And as for reading: "Read Linnaeus. Not for botany. Read him because he never used an inexact word." That was the trouble with the whole damned educational system. All this bilge, and the universities can't turn out a college senior who can write a coherent sentence.

Reading this over, I doubt that I have said much of anything new about Ezra Pound. I can remember, as a child, a certain ballroom adorned by a multi-faceted chandelier, formed of a hundred tiny mirrors, which revolved slowly in the glow of colored spotlights. Pound's mind spins and refracts in the same way. Or to shift the simile, his speech is like the focusing of a ground-glass camera: The subject is always there, but now it is blurred, now sharp, now vaguely defined. He loves talk, and this mistress may yet prove his undoing, for his tongue is unbridled, and sly, deceitful men will ride his improprieties for all the embarrassment that can be drawn from them. And Pound, to recall his criticism of Eliot, also is hurt by the company he keeps, he swims with the grand abandon of an ancient shark, but a host of parasitic pilot fish ride on his back. So far, he is not disposed to shake them off.

That Pound, as an American citizen, made some imprudent broadcasts from Italy during the war years, is plain enough. By nice legal definition, perhaps these exhortations gave enough curious aid and comfort to the enemy to constitute treason to the United States, though two hours with Pound are enough to prompt grave doubts on this score; one envisions Bill Mauldin's Buck and Willy listening to Pound on the short-wave.

Whatever these sins may have been, they are long past; the nation has forgiven worse offenders. Pound now has served twelve years as a political prisoner in a land that prides itself on political freedom, and it seems to me good that at long last, this old Ulysses will go back to Rapallo, there to lie in a raft on the infinite sea, and gaze at the infinite sky.

All too soon it was time to pick up my wife and my sister, Mrs. William H. Evans, and return to the club for dinner. Pound was tiring, but the guests were reluctant to let him go. As I drew him and Fred Grab toward the door, he was deep in conversation with Miss Kohler about the "Va. ¼'ly," which he had dreams of reshaping into an international literary journal. He was drawn to the magazine for a number of reasons. He identified it with Charlottesville, Monticello, the University of Virginia, and Thomas Jefferson. More importantly, I think, since Noel Stock's little magazine, *Edge*, had folded, he needed an outlet. But nothing came of this dream.

Once at "St. Liz" when it was bitter cold outdoors and we were forced to huddle in a dirty corner of Chestnut Ward, I had said to the poet (only half believing myself), "One day before long we will sit at the feet of Jefferson's statue in the Rotunda Club and eat spoon bread and Smithfield ham." But here we were, before just such a dinner, adorned by a steaming dish of snaps cooked with ham. Just as we were finishing the soup the headwaiter, Washington, known to three generations of Richmonders, whispered in my ear, "Mr. Meacham, dat gentman have to wear a coat." Since the poet had declined to wear his coat when we left the house, I had no intention of making an issue of it now. And so I whispered back, "Washington, you tell the manager to record in the annals of the staid old Rotunda that the only gentleman ever to eat in the dining room without a coat was Ezra Pound." He thought about this for a moment, then asked, "Who he?" Later, when Washington had read the *News-Leader* story, his dignity was restored, and I was again permitted to occupy my favorite table at Jefferson's feet.

The next morning my wife served sally lunn muffins, and the poet was delighted. He had not had such food in thirteen years; no, not even at the club. As he was eating his fifth (at Lucy's insistence), he glanced up and asked, "Are these the last?" When she assured him there were several in the kitchen he said, "Fine, I want to take them to Dorothy." And he did, holding them in his hands, like so many eggs, all the way to Washington. From time to time he mentioned "sally-Olunn" in his letters from Italy. Later, Lucy mailed the recipe to Mrs. Pound but I never learned how the Italian cooks made out with it.

About ten in the morning he kissed the ladies goodbye, and we returned to Washington. There is no doubt that my wife was uneasy about his visit. Many poets had visited us, but, as she remarked, "I've never entertained a genius." And there were, undeniably, certain unusual circumstances. But she was just herself, and the poet was completely won over. In fact, he referred to her in his last letters to me.

Meantime, what most of us assumed was a routine interview of a visiting celebrity turned out to be the scoop of the year.

Mr. Friddell's story, which was front-page news in the *News-Leader*, was picked up by the wire services and sent around the world, and portions of it were broadcast from England and Canada. And so, all day, as I was driving Pound and Grab back to Washington, my telephones, office and home, were ringing. Pound was big news. The literary editor of one of the wire services finally got in touch with me when I returned that night. He said he wanted to do a long and sympathetic interview. He had been in touch with the poet's publisher, New Directions, and seemed desperately anxious to reach Ezra. I told him I would convey his message to Pound, which I did, but he ignored this and all other requests from newspapers and magazines.

It is not hard to understand why he should be cynical about this sudden interest. He might very well have said with Dr. Johnson, "had it been early, it had been kind."

I thought Mr. Friddell's interview could not have been improved upon, and it certainly was sympathetic, yet Pound was both suspicious and critical of all newspapermen. He had been quoted as saying, "Yeats is a much better writer than I am." In the following letter he corrects that "unintentional attribution of false modesty." Mr. Friddell also falls into the common error of labeling Pound's Rome broadcasts as being *for* Italy's wartime Fascist government when the poet insists (and the record shows) he broadcast for himself as an American citizen. It is not difficult to understand why many would consider the distinction unimportant. After all, he did make the broadcasts. But the facts are that he sought the microphone for what he considered his duty.

Pound's reference to Eliot and "future felicities" springs from our conversation about a program for The Poetry Society of Virginia. I had corresponded with Mr. Eliot, and had offered him $1,000 to read at our annual meeting at William and Mary College. Pound was trying to raise money for his fare to Italy, but the best I could do was to arrange, tentatively, for a series of lectures through the University Center in Richmond at $100 a day. Understandably, he was not interested in accepting less than we offered T. S. Eliot.

(28)

May 2, 1958

DEAR MEACHAM

Thanks for yrs of the whatever and the encloseures.

Let us CORRECT at once Mr. Friddell's unintentional attribution of false modesty, to your and their correspondent.

I did NOT say that Yeats was a better writer than I am, or was.

Friddell is an excellent reporter with an almost perfect verbal memory but he missed the connecting words,

I was quoting Ford Madox Ford, who said, i.e. FORD said, "Of course Yeats is a much greater POET than I am, BUT he is a gargoyle."

Get the EXACT shade. Ford did not say BETTER poet, he most certainly and ABsolutely did NOT think Yeats a better WRITER

His words were what he meant, i.e.

a GREATER POET

adjective *greater*, noun POET

****

More serious is the statement that I broadcast FOR the wartime fascist government,

It took me, I think it was, TWO years insistence and wrangling etc to GET HOLD of their microphone, and repeat time and TIME again,

This is what Brooks Adams said in 1903 or *this is what B. Adams* PRINTED in 1897

CAN this be axis propaganda??

***

Coming to future felicities, WHAT could Eliot do for your poetry society that I can't?

Marcella is coming to Richmond on or about the 17th inst. she could import and export D. P. and myself, saving you making two trips, to Washington and back,

Would that be too soon to rake in the price of steamship tickets, by answering the questions in yr letter publicly TO the assembled eggheads and leaders of the Southern poetic renaissance.

At any rate I haven't time to answer 'em in this letter, which will be posted tomorrow and possibly reach you by Tuesday.

best to the ladies gawd bless 'em

                                                                    E. P.

Pound refers to May 17, the date of the annual meeting of The Poetry Society of Virginia, when Richard Wilbur was to read. Pound made a brief stopover in Richmond en route to Virginia Beach for a short visit with his friend Robert Furniss. Hugh Kenner wrote me of Guy Davenport's account of Pound, "on the beach, wrapped in blankets, by a fire, gazing long, returned Odysseus, at the loudsounding sea."

During his short stay in Richmond I drove Pound to the Richmond *News-Leader* office to see Mr. Kilpatrick about his credentials as a "foreign correspondent" for the paper. I was surprised to hear him ask for "credentials" also for Miss Marcella Spann, since this was the first intimation I had that she planned to accompany the Pounds to Italy.

Marcella Spann was a young and attractive schoolteacher in Washington who was a frequent visitor at St. Elizabeths. During the early months of 1958, while Pound was getting *Thrones* ready for New Directions, he was also working on an anthology of which she is listed as co-editor. The collection, *Confucius to Cummings* (New Directions) finally appeared in 1964. The dust jacket stated that "this anthology is Ezra Pound's own choice of the poetry of various ages and cultures. . . ." Actually, the poet had never cared much for anthologies, since the occasion many years ago when his offer to edit an anthology in which every poem would represent an invention was declined. Once I asked him if he had read a multivolumed collection by two distinguished editors (one a very close friend) I had seen among his effects. He replied, contemptuously, "I'd rather read a telephone directory."

(29)

6th Maggio 1958

Dear H. M.

If the 17th is out per Wilbur, I don't see how to save you at least ONE transport.

i.e. Marcella cd/ bring us DOWN and you wd/ have to bring us back.

The 17th was aimed at saving you milege on the roads.

Nope, not interested in lecture tours or courses.

It was only the fee offered Eliot that aroused my greed.

and naturally not interested in WORKING

let alone at 8% the possumic rate.

thanks for PILOT clipping which I will peruse in bus on way to next scrable.

Saluti alle gent/ me dignore.

Yrs

E. P.

(30)

3514 Brothers Place   Washington, D. C.

18 May 1958

Dear Meacham

Just seen Kilpatrick in *National Review,* probably better if I don't come back to Richmond
I don't want to get you into a jam,
Might be better to let well enough alone

I hope J. J. K[ilpatrick] will come thru with some sort of credentials

                not that he need print any news from Europe.

   Might be helpful if he said what the paper
[*Richmond News-Leader*] does NOT want in the way of foreign items.

Cordially yours

      E. P.

and best to the ladies.

In the following letters Pound refers to Dr. W. Melville Jones, Dean of the College of William and Mary (a good friend of mine and of poetry) and to last-minute plans for a trip to Williamsburg. I was not worried about his getting me into a "jam." On the contrary, I was honored to have him, and I especially wanted Dorothy to come to Virginia where she has so many Tucker relatives. I had planned to bring them to Richmond, but unexpected guests arrived, and we went to the Williamsburg Inn at Williamsburg for a weekend.

(31)

                            21 Maggio 1958

DEAR H. M.

   Apart from a few serious items like saving what is left of our BLOODIED country from the scum of Moscow and FDR's vermin/

am more concerned with getting Marcella's anthology in order to send to New Directions/
   (silence reigns re/ light penetrating the Va/ ¼ly)
and getting packed/

AND getting her car sold so she will have a few stray bucks when she gets to YuRupp/

She may bring us down to Va/ IF room in her sister's domicile/ on 29th or zummat.

Has Dun & Bradstreet any means of watching over used car vendor who won't remove her eyeteeth in exchange?

Dates for Williamsburg dont seem much imperriled?

D. P. and I could presumably be on tap for the 31/ to the 32nd
(alias primo giugho.)

and it wdn't much matter whence you plucked us up,
or whether you brought one or both of us back to Wash.

Marcella suspended between exams/ and fambly/

Where do you plan to start FROM to git to Wash/ by NINE
o'clock (you do NOT say whether A.M. or P.M.?

(I won't be in Wash on June 7th tho D. P. may.)

I mean I presumably wd/ be at Va/beach on that date/ and D. P.
in Wash/ ergo the 31 sounds more likely COMBINATION.

Is Kilpat/ comin thru with his letter of credentials or invite.
His owner needn't know it exists.

Yrz   E. P.

Order of importance in my present scheme of existence.

   A. D. P.'s convenience
   B. Marcella's idem
   C. my amusement, or serious activity
                 as circs permit

Is Jones interested in SERIOUSLY delousing
the teaching of literature in our infected
institutions for the murder of life of the
mind?

There is nothing I care less to meet than profs/ *contented* with
       the present state of degradation in their
                     sources of income.

I see the London Times printed a note on April 4th
Suggesting how callow egotists cd/ save otiose postal
expenses

E. P.

I mean, am glad to see *you*. If Jones ain't DISgusted, I don't want
to meet him. I value Kilpatrick's warning against incompre-
henders.

(32)

17 May/ 3514 BROTHERS PLACE
WASH D.C.

DEAR MEACHAM

What are your approximate conveniences as from June 1st/ to
12th/??

      conveyance, shelter etc in Richmond, or at
circumjacence.

I want to be taken to and fetched from Va. Beach at some time
in that interval

Probably start trek toward port of embarkation about June 25.
all very whirlagig, but passport fotos have been tuʞ

A Not sure of behavior and schedule of Marcella's bro/ in law/

B Furniss at Va. Beach presumably amenable to reason.
                                    (i.e. re/
chronology of June.

                Rip van Wunkle in whirligig/

some beautiful items in european press, of course
highly inaccurate, but joyful in general.

                    best to the ladies

                    Yours

                    E. P.

H. M.

    Repeat WHERE are you starting FROM on Saturday the 31st/??
as I may be in Richmond, I cd/ accompany you to Brothers Place
IF you are starting from Richmond?

Not interested in anything but agenda.

I take it Va ¼ ly / News Leader
have done all they can.

E. P.

23 Maggio

(33)

26 May 1958

Dear Meacham

O.K. I will be in Washington, so you can come Friday. repose tranquilly in the nation's kepperti

Perhaps it would be more convenient to collect me first and D. P. second.

I am (for your private eye and ear, at 2407 Fifteenth St. N. W. apartment 511 top floor opposite elevator)

Thanks and sorry for all the uncertainties and wobbles

E. P.

c/o C. La Drière
2407 15th St.
Washington N. W. DC.

(34)

15 June (1958)

Dear H. M.

I see Va. Un. has supressed one rag, and the prex resigned.
Can you persuade Wyllie to WRITE to
La Drière,
N. H. Pearson
J. Theobald, 1390 Merrit Drive, El Cajan, Calif.

re/ the utility, not to say NEED of a forum, even of 8 pages tho why not 16, IN some regular periodical

where error wd/ be corrected,

even if not 100% wrong, EVEN if only 5% wrong.

and where knowledge of state of MIND among the intelligent wd/ be kept up to date.

as per example: re/ Waddell, Rock, Goullart as sources.

re/ Blocker, Kenner, even E. Miner as reporters ON the PRESENT
                    as distinct from 1954
                                                    state of the more lively
perceptions.

I hark back to three books recd. on three successive days
        a few weeks ago.

Kilpatrick saw the desirability of such a forum/

the profs/ agree with him that a magazine like the Va. ¼
would reach people whom a weekly page in the *News Leader*
would not. which is not against Wyllie's starting on his own in
the News Lr OR better, using it as a place to report on the section
of the

Quarterly WHEN and/or if.

Whether Melville J. wd/ also support Wyllie?? You can tell
better than I.

The NEED of facing clear definations/ emphasized by recent letters
recd. by E. P.

                    that is to say, numerous blokes with names, do not,
and will not, and possibly CANNOT define anything.

                                        and without definition
no science, no knowledge, no history.

                                                    yrs.

                                                    E. P.

You might phone Wyllie
                    one or 2 11

    My son-in-law, Lieutenant Colonel John C. McWhorter,
is a philatelist, and I thought it might be helpful if I could
start for him a collection of stamps commemorating poets.
Mrs. Pound mentions this in the following letter, as well as
fluoridation of the water supply which she, along with my
sister Mrs. Joseph Walker, opposed.

June '58

Dear Mr. Meacham,

Thanking you again for such an interesting week-end. We both enjoyed it so much.

Ezra has sent one of his books to the old lady at St. George T's House. My copy of the booklet goes, marked, to a friend in London who knows about St. G.

I am enclosing a copy of the English "Housewives" on fluoridation: they have been fighting several years on that, unpoisoned bread etc:

I do not have any "poet" stamps at present but will bear in mind. "Animals" I could supply? Not to the same point.

Hope you got home comfortably.

"saluti cordiali" as the wops say.

Dorothy Pound

This was the height of the season at Williamsburg, and to further complicate matters, Virginia was celebrating the 350th anniversary of the first permanent English settlement in America at Jamestown, less than fifteen miles from the Inn. When I called for reservations I found they had been sold out months in advance. Fortunately, Dr. Jones used his considerable influence and arranged for excellent rooms on forty-eight hours' notice.

Ezra was staying with Professor La Drière of The Catholic University of America, so I picked him up first, then drove across town to Brothers Place for Dorothy. We enjoyed a leisurely drive in beautiful spring weather, with a stopover at Fredericksburg for a visit to James Madison's law office. We reached Williamsburg Inn at about 2:00 P.M., somewhat before checkout time, so we had to wait in the lobby. That is, Dorothy and I waited. Ezra found a sofa in the East Lounge and slept peacefully in spite of the hum of conversation and the hustle and bustle of departing guests.

After an hour's rest the Pounds met me in the lobby, where

we were to meet Melville and Helen Jones. Ezra walked out
to the beautiful front lawn and, attracted by the warm sun
and the soft grass, stretched out for another rest. I either had
to stand there looking down on him, or join him, so I laid
down beside him and we talked until the Joneses arrived.

We drove to Jamestown, then returned for a tour of the
Governor's Palace and other historic buildings. The St.
George Tucker house was not open to the public because
Mrs. Mary H. Coleman, a Tucker, still owned and occupied
the eighteenth-century dwelling, but since Dorothy is herself
a Tucker, Dr. Jones arranged for a brief visit. It was only as
we were leaving that Mrs. Coleman realized who Pound was,
and throughout much of the visit she had chatted about the
time Robert Frost had visited her. Dorothy was much interested in photographs of her Virginia relatives.

We had dinner at the Kings Arms Tavern with the Joneses
and Professor William E. McBurney as our guests. I realized
almost at once that this was a mistake, for while the food
(Smithfield ham and sally lunn) was superb, the chit-chat
bothered the poet. They seemed anxious to return to Washington and so the next morning after they had breakfast in
their room we left, again in beautiful weather.

Dorothy sat beside me and the poet reclined on the back
seat, asleep, or half asleep. He could not get enough rest and
so I thought of the line in Canto 83: "There is fatigue deep
as the grave." And I recalled the unforgettable line, which I
quoted aloud: "In the gloom the gold gathers the light about
it." I was thinking of the aging poet, free at last. While he
would never visit the Altar of heaven, he would return to
Italy where he was first drawn by Dante and where his
daughter and his grandchildren awaited him. He must have
shared my thoughts for he said, almost in a whisper, "In the
gloom . . ." and added, "I'd like to take you there with me,
Meacham." "There" being the mausoleum of Galla Placidia,
Roman Empress, just behind San Vitale, in Ravenna, Italy,

where by design, or chance, or daily miracle of the Saint, the gold of the ceiling catches, and for a moment holds, the last rays of the sun. Then he spoke no more. *"Era l'ora che il disio."* It was the hour that homeward turns the thought.

Pound's fortitude throughout the years of his imprisonment is well-known, but little has been written about his wife, Dorothy Shakespear Pound. She was the Penelope of this modern Odyssey, or, to put a better word to it, she was the Saint of Saint Elizabeths. In writing to me about her visits with Ezra and Dorothy during that bitter time, Marianne Moore was impressed by Pound's "resilience of mind, his obedience to regulations. Mrs. Pound's selfless . . . service to E. P. left an ineffable impression on me of nobility—of wholesomeness and of self-sacrifice. . . ." Dorothy not only waited, she also served, always at the poet's side during visiting hours, helping him set up camp on the lawn during warm weather, greeting visitors and, in general, playing hostess in a medieval madhouse as if it were a London drawing room. She is a gifted woman; intelligent, well informed, and a brilliant conversationalist, yet once Ezra was fairly launched she fell silent.

During our drive to Washington from Williamsburg on that bright May morning she talked (after much prompting) about her childhood in London. Later, during our correspondence after she had returned to Italy, she filled in a few blank spots, although she much preferred to write about Ezra and their son Omar and his family. She was born in London on September 14, 1886, the daughter of Henry Hope ("always called Hope," she said) and Olivia Tucker Shakespear. Most of the Shakespears distinguished themselves in the Indian Civil Service, but her father was a solicitor in London, where she grew up.

Pound had written, "My wife's connections go back to that Tucker who married John Randolph's ma and brought out a Blackstone," and since the Tuckers are to Virginia what the Lowells are to Massachusetts I wanted to know more about this relationship. She thought the Tucker who edited the Blackstone was a first cousin of her grandfather's father. This was St. George Tucker (1752-1827) who was born in Bermuda and brought to Virginia as a child. He practiced law in Williamsburg, served in the Colonial Army during the Revolutionary War, and was either a state or a federal judge during the remainder of his distinguished career. At the time of his death he was judge of the U. S. District Court, District of Virginia. He published an annotated edition of *Blackstone's Commentaries* in 1803.

William Tucker, a Norman yeoman, crossed the Channel with William the Conqueror and established the family in England. In her book, *St. George Tucker, Citizen of No Mean City*, Mrs. Mary H. Coleman (who had entertained us at Williamsburg) wrote, "When George Tucker of Milton married Frances St. George about 1600 he introduced into the family a combination of names which have become famous in England, India, Bermuda, and America." In five generations of American Tuckers there were eight judges or professors of law, twelve editors or authors, six clergymen, three of whom became bishops, including Henry St. George Tucker who was at one time Presiding Bishop of the Episcopal Church, U. S. A.

Mrs. Pound said her mother knew William Butler Yeats "about 1888 or so," and she remembers him coming to tea when she was four or five years old. They were probably introduced by the poet Lionel Pigot Johnson, a cousin of Mrs. Shakespear, a friend of Yeats and fellow member of the Rhymers' Club. He was devoted to Dorthy and wrote a long poem for her, "Lines to a Lady upon Her Third Birthday," which begins: "Dear Cousin, to be three years old,/ Is to have found the age of gold." Yeats fell in love with Olivia, and some of his loveliest lyrics were written to her. However, she married Hope Shakespear, and Yeats pursued for years the lovely Maud Gonne, one of the heroines of the Irish "troubles." He later married Georgia Hyde-Lees, a friend of Olivia's.

Dorothy's mother, who had written several novels, moved in the best London literary circles, and it was at a tea for American writers that she met Ezra and asked him to call at her home at Brunswick Gardens. It was there that he met Dorothy. She has been described as beautiful by all who knew her then, and she was still beautiful when I saw her last in 1958, when she was seventy.

Olivia, her daughter Dorothy, and Ezra frequently attended Yeats's teas (she referred to them in her letters to me as "W. B. Y's Monday Evenings"), and it was through the Shakespears that Pound was drawn into the Yeats circle. Ezra was short on funds, as usual, and so he contracted to give a series of lectures on medieval poets. Dorothy and her mother were among those present at what Dorothy described as "a most dreary place, The Polytechnic, in London."

Dorothy and Ezra were married in 1914 with Yeats as best man. Pound returned the compliment when Yeats married some years later. At about this time Dorothy turned to painting and might well have had a career of her own. She wrote me that she came under the influence of Wyndham Lewis and adopted his forms to simple landscapes. Omar now has her paintings, and there is some talk of getting out a small book of prints. Dorothy sent me two original watercolors from Rapallo, one a Roman scene painted in 1925, and the other a mountainscape of the Dolomites, at Bolzano. She wrote that in 1930, Hours Press in Paris published a limited edition of *A Draft of XXX Cantos* "For which I did some fancy caps, but without any illustrations across them."

In London and Paris, and later at Rapallo, she shared Ezra's intellectual life and was much admired by Pound's friends. Most of the time they lived in hotels: "I never cared for cooking," she said. The years slipped by and then came

the terrible experience of Pisa and St. Elizabeths. She told me
many times she did not want anything written about the
years at the hospital, but every book and almost every article
about the poet published since 1946 has described the poet
at "St. Liz." Dorothy devoted all her time and energies to
Pound's affairs, literary and financial. Ezra's funds were
seized when he was arrested, and she had the same experience
because the government considered her an alien, although
by marriage she was, and is, an American citizen.

The poet's very able attorney, Julien Cornell, soon arranged
to have Dorothy appointed as "committee" of the person and
the property of her husband, by the District of Columbia
Court. With Dorothy's funds in England impounded by the
British government, and Ezra's bank account in Pennsylvania
blocked by the Alien Property Custodian (although they
were not aliens), they were in urgent need of funds for their
attorney. Mr. Cornell explains how this was solved "quite
unexpectedly." On November 29, 1945 he called on poet
E. E. Cummings and his wife to report on the situation and
mentioned the shortage of funds. Cummings immediately
handed him a check for $1,000, saying, "I sold a painting last
week and don't need the money. Please take it and use it for
Ezra." Dorothy later repaid Cummings, although he had
intended it as a gift. (When Pound returned to Italy in 1958
he worried needlessly about money, and Ernest Hemingway
getting word of it, sent him a check for $1,500. Ezra canceled
it on the face, and had it set in plastic and used it for a paper-
weight. Dorothy recently wrote that it is still at the castle in
Brunnenburg.)

Mrs. Pound lived in a damp basement apartment in south-
east Washington, a short distance from the hospital. During
the thirteen years she spent her mornings writing letters and
attending to their business affairs and in the afternoons, rain
or shine, she was with Ezra. In writing about the lost years
she often adds, "Poor Ezra." When I think of them, I say,

"Poor Dorothy." But she held her head high, and neither wanted people to be concerned about their personal sorrows. She did not care that the public thought Ezra insane (his writings during his confinement would give the lie to that), but she did resent statements that Pound was a Fascist (he never was) and that he had broadcast *for* the Mussolini regime (he did not).

With many Tucker cousins in Virginia, and sharing Ezra's great admiration for Thomas Jefferson and the University of Virginia, Dorthy hoped the Pound papers, valued at several hundred thousand dollars, would eventually find their way to the Rare Book Room of the Alderman Library. She also knew that my collection of Poundiana had been presented to the university some years before. Few items in the poet's collection are more interesting than the Ernest Fenollosa papers, turned over to Pound by the scholar's widow in 1913, and which had a tremendous impact on Pound's poetry and his thinking. When Hugh Kenner visited the Pounds at Schloss Brunnenburg in 1964, he was permitted to go through the Pound collection (one of the few accorded this honor), and he conceived the idea of having the Fenollosa papers microfilmed for the University of Virginia Library (he was there for two years as visiting lecturer and had fallen in love with the town, the university, and the people). The microfilming never was completed and so Dorothy laboriously copied in longhand, several of the notebooks and Noh plays that have not been published, and sent them along to me suggesting that I present them to the University of Virginia.

I sincerely hope that when her son Omar publishes a volume of her watercolors he will include a biography, for she deserves a book of her own. There are many anecdotes in her letters that are a part of the literary history of our times. I cannot resist the temptation to record at least one. In July, 1946, she was desperately anxious to get her passport renewed so she could be with Ezra in Washington where, for all she knew, he would soon go on trial for his life. Here is her cryptic account of a conversation with two officials. "Anecdote:—(a) You must give the name and date of sailing before we give you a passport. (b) You must have a passport before we give you a sailing."

Mrs. Pound's responsibilities as "committee" for the poet have weighed heavily upon her in recent years, for she has been involved in establishing a trust fund for Pound as well as in the final disposition of his papers.[4] Once trustees have been appointed and the problem of the papers worked out, she can lay aside the burden she has carried for so many years. Now, as these lines are written, she is eighty, and tired. She divides her time between visiting their son Omar, at present in England, staying with Mary in the castle near Merano and, as weather worsens she returns to her room in the Albergo Italia, Rapallo, with a balcony looking down on the sea.

As last-minute details were being worked out in connection with the court hearing there was much talk of post-liberation plans. Many people in high places who wanted Pound released did not know whether he was sane or insane, or what he might do once he was out of custody. One suggested a small place in the South where the Pounds would be out of the public eye. Another felt Pound should be in an inconspicuous place where he could be visited regularly by a physician (a psychiatrist?) with implications that he should not be officially released. However, I believe Ezra and Dorothy had decided some weeks before he was released to return to Italy. There were compelling reasons for this: The grandchildren were there, both had close ties with Italy and England, it was less expensive, and they were wanted. I am sure the happiest years of their lives were spent in Rapallo, and their travels bring them back there at least once every year.

There was more than the usual amount of red tape in getting

passports, and it was the end of June before all details had
been worked out. In the interval the Pounds were pretty
much at loose ends. There had been the three visits to
Virginia previously described, and Ezra lived some time in
the apartment of Professor La Drière, since Dorothy's apartment on Brothers Place was much too small for two people.
While his poetry is required reading in every university,
there were no invitations for the poet to speak. I suppose it
is understandable, in the context of events, that people were
not anxious to entertain the Pounds.

While they were waiting, James Laughlin, the poet's
friend and publisher, came to Washington to see what he
could do, and, with La Drière accompanied Pound to a
studio where he made three one-hour recordings. And then
it was time to go. David Horton and his wife drove the
Pounds to New York "in three stages" as Dorothy described
the last weekend in America in a letter to Dr. Giovannini.
They visited Ezra's childhood home in Wyncote, Pennsylvania "which has been nicely painted and furnished. E. P.
remarked that Isabel (Mrs. P. Senior) would have greatly
approved it all. Then two nights at a swank swimming-pool-
tennis-court old house. Then chez W. C. W. . . . . Bill sweet
as ever." They spent two nights at the home of Pound's
old friend Dr. William Carlos Williams at Rutherford, New
Jersey, and they were joined there by their son Omar who
accompanied them aboard the "Christoforo Colombo." Others
in the party included Marcella Spann and Professor Norman
Holmes Pearson. Reporters swarmed around Ezra as they
had since the day of his release, but in her boat-letter to
Giovannini dated July 2, 1958 and mailed at Gibraltar,
Dorothy said, "Omar kept all the press from our cabin."

PART FOUR

WHEN THE POUND PARTY LANDED in Italy, the poet gave the Fascist salute by way of thumbing his nose at America, thus convincing a few more million of his fellow citizens that he was, after all, a member of the party, although there is proof beyond his own categorical statement that he was not.[1] He made a few indiscreet remarks he would later regret, and he was asked the usual silly questions. (Sample: "How is it that you who merited fame as a seer did not see?") The party—Dorothy, Ezra, and Marcella Spann—went directly from Genoa to Schloss Brunnenburg near Merano, in the Italian Alps, where they were welcomed by the poet's daughter Princess Mary de Rachewiltz, her husband, Prince Boris, and their two children, Patricia and Walter.

After a few weeks rest Pound was ready to resume work on the final series of the *Cantos*,[2] and he was given the Roman tower of the castle for his study. Most writers engaged in a work of such magnitude would have found time and energy for little else, but the poet continued to sound off when he heard or read anything that ran counter to his agenda; that is, his views on education, usury, and the Constitution of the United States. "He will hew to the line of right, let the chips fall where they may." Something prompted him to air his views on American universities in a letter to *Illustrazione Italiana* in September 1958. Apparently this was picked up by someone in the American Embassy in Rome and sent to Washington, with some critical comments. Pound heard of it and fired off a letter to Secretary of State Herter. This communication is interesting, not only for its contents, but because it provides an insight into the ability of the "mad poet" to cerebrate and summarize. His argument is cogent and persuasive.

Pound is disturbed, as he has been since his own college years, that American youth is taught a type of United States

history which makes no reference to who controls the issue
of money.[3] Again and again he goes back to the Constitution
and the clause which gives Congress, the representative of
the people, the right to coin money and determine its value.
This monopoly, according to Pound, Congress is bound by
the Constitution to exercise directly. Instead, the Nineteenth
Congress handed this power over to private banks, which
policy Benton opposed; hence, in the *Cantos*, Thomas Hart
Benton is a hero. Conversely, President Woodrow Wilson is
a villain for permitting establishment of the Federal Reserve
Bank, to Pound, federal in name only. He complains that our
young people are not taught that the treasury issues interest-
bearing bonds, sold to commercial banks through the Federal
Reserve for the purpose of putting money into circulation, so
that most of the money we have, has back of it, bonds, the
interest of which is paid by taxes to private banks. For the
people to pay interest to banks for the credit they already
have; that is, which pre-exists the issue of bonds, is to Pound
a neat trick. To the objection that the interest is paid for a
kind of middle-man service, Pound's answer is (in the
Cantos) non-interest bearing bonds on public credit. The
poet's letter to the Secretary of State follows:

DEAR MR. HERTER   14 September 1958

I am informed that some subhuman ape in our embassy in
Rome has stated that I have been making derogatory remarks
about the U.S.

I have no means of verifying this statement, but may say in
this connection that a certain Cose-schi has invited me to lecture
or was suggesting that I do so, and that I have declined, as I
needed three months rest. I have also declined invitations to speak
on Canada Radio, and am declining an invitation to speak on
the British Radio.

I would point out, vide enclosure [reprint of *Illustrazione*
letter] that objection to the state of american universities, specif-
icly for their neglect of U.S. History does not constitute an

attack on the U.S. but is rather a defense of what decency there is left in our country.

If some of the minor officials in your department consider the study of american history as aid and comfort to Moscow, that again displays a state of mind that might, or even should, arouse curiosity.

Cordially yours

EZRA POUND

The following hand-written note refers to a bright red woolen sport shirt I sent Pound on his birthday. In letter No. 36 the poet mentions another shirt in which he was photographed many times.

(35)

(undated)

MEACHAM

As to
political significance of yr choice of color?
in excitable segment of Europe!!

E. P.

(36)

H. M.   *(undated)*

I wuz naked and yu clothed me. The ole lady who copies shirts from Wing's design (Wing of London to impress brit/snobs) is DEElighted with my summer order, BUT there is still room for the u.s. contingent, and I send thanks in anticipation.

Yrs/ as recd/ in Tirolo
has had more publicity, foto/pbcty than any other in my long career. etc.

benedictions

E. P.

(37)

5 Dec '58

DEAR MEACHAM

Thanks for splendours, splendour of shirt, WITH directions. Directions for ham,

still in mythological area. Am. Heritage number whatever.

Copies of alledged verifax series have not yet arrived.

Need of staff and a dynamo.
                              best wishes for Xmas.

Mary having been intent on MY glories has greatly neglected to inform me of extent of Boris'[4] work.

I don't know what I can do about it. If you know of anyone interested in AGriculture?

    etc. and history?

They pay to illustrate King Geo's statue, but information that wd/ be useful drives 'em to allergy.

                              and so forth,
news of election in the U. S. still very sparse here.

                    ever yours

                    E. P.

Hope Kilpatric shows you fotostat re/ Jefferson in our era.

As Wyndham Lewis said, "Pound's letters are a pedagogic volcano." Most poets are prolific letter-writers, and Pound was no exception. His mail was always a source of great pleasure, but now that he was in Italy, in poor health, and working with almost maniacal intensity to finish the *Cantos* it was becoming increasingly difficult for him to communicate with his friends in America and England.

To remove this bottleneck I offered to have our Dun & Bradstreet office in Richmond reproduce such letters to me and to others as he wanted distributed to those with whom he was currently corresponding.

(38)

(undated)

H. M. for verifax/ list as per enc.

1. Do you know anyone sufficiently interested in problem of translation, and FLOOD of inferior brain wash now offered as such to write to Dr. Rudolph Stamm
56 Willadingweg, Berne, Switzerland re/ his article in
Neue Zuricher Zeitung, 8 Feb

OR to look it up in the files of that paper.

2. Anyone object to system which nevr prints the man, but only what someone, unusually un- or poorly qualified says ABOUT him, usually with effort to distract from senso morale (vid. Dante D. V. E. or WHY he wrote at all)

3. Any objection to there being NO periodical in the U. S. where E. P. can CONSECUTIVELY communicate even with the few hundred people who are interested.

Impossible to subscribe to all papers where ONE isolated note appears.

Also doubt if Univ. Libs/ CAN mobilize quick enough to subscribe to useful european papers BEFORE it is too late.

Note MacMillan advance to C. Norman for book ABOUT E. P.

F. Reis wanting to publish letters to Joyce, mostly before 1920??
all of which distracts from ideas and news needed NOW/

4. any objection to there being, as far as I can make out, NO

writers of known position who will face ideas E. P.

now considers worth a fight either FOR or even ABOUT.

Anonymous "Spectator" one sheet leaflet, printed without

address   Provincetown R.I.

11   Caffe   Dec and Jan.   67 via della Croce, Roma.

Cultura nel mondo, (Carucci) Viale Guilio Cesare 51. a. Roma
essential note on Canto 95 is in Meridiano d' Italia, 10 Feb (1959)

ALL books or articles worth notice can (and/or SHD) be sent to

M. Oberti, via Montallegro   32 (a 43)

GENOVA

Papal note in anon. Spect. worth attention

Odlin reprints note from Townsman.

Libraries LACK work by, and comments on, Allan Upward and
B. [asil] Bunting[5]

5.   ANY objection to Arlington meeting shouting down Horton
because he was YEARS ago associated with Kasper when K/was
selecting Agassiz, seldom in agreement with K, even at that time.

I had written the poet that my daughter was in Nuremberg
where her husband was stationed, and said she might call on
his publisher in Munich. He set me straight on that point
and does some checking on the list of those to receive the
verifax copies of his communiques. The letter is undated.

(39)

(undated)

DEAR MEACHAM

Not publisher / translator in Munich.[6] Have sent address to yr
daughter. Thanks offer to verifax my letters./ Will tell following to send you copies of material for redistribution. Think you
have addresses of

N. H. Pearson
Horton
Giovannini
LaDrière

Please add

Fred Grab, 1717 A Parker St., Berkeley, Calif. Reno Odlin Gig Harbor, Washington; Dr. Vincent Miller, Spartanburg, South Carolina.

I wonder if Mrs. Cabell would like copies?

                    Unless marked urgent you cd wait until two or three pages before posting.

To save time for England suggest you send several copies to William Cookson, 5 Cranbourne Ct. Albert Bridge Road. London SW 11 for redistribution to Merchant, Stock and Swabey.

                        y.v.t.

                        E. P.

as many copies as you like for reserve but *not* to distribute to undependables.

Dr. Leo Charles Donnelly mentioned in the following letter (No. 40), died at the home of a daughter in Dansville, Michigan on May 30, 1958. During World War I, he served with distinction as an orthopedic surgeon in France. In 1935 he founded the short-lived Social Credit party in Detroit, a political group which advocated federal government financing of individuals, private businesses, and industry. He was considered a crackpot, although within fifteen years the Small Business Administration and other government agencies had advanced hundreds of millions of dollars to help finance small businesses. In 1944 Dr. Donnelly was presidential candidate for the Greenback party. Throughout his career he was at odds with the Wayne County Medical Society, for he was a noncomformist like his friend Ezra Pound, and he was once expelled, but was later reinstated. At the time of his death, Dr. Donnelly was planning to run for Congress.

George Dillon, one of America's best lyric poets, was awarded the Pulitzer Prize in 1932 for his second collection, *The Flowering Stone*. He collaborated with Edna St. Vincent

Millay in translating Baudelaire's *Flowers of Evil*, and in 1961 his translation, *Three Plays of Racine*, appeared. He was associated with Harriet Monroe, publisher of *Poetry*, *A Magazine of Verse*, and was for a time its editor.

George had written to me about an account of Pound's visit to Richmond, and commented on the "sanctimonious inanities" that were published about the poet. He also wrote that "His noble bearing and indomitable spirt in misfortune have made him a greater figure than before." I mentioned this in my next letter to Pound. His reply, humorous at first, develops into an interesting commentary on his relations with Miss Monroe and *Poetry*.

(40)

HOTEL GRANDE ITALIA   22 Marzo '59

DEAR H. M.

Yepp/ I done heer of ole Georgie Dillon, wot never done me no good while he was editor of Harriet's Handkerchief.

I never tho't him venal / and I dont spose he is to blame fer getting the SPEWlitzer
                    which is NOT what I wd/ remember any man by
er for having
it handed to him.

                    As to the history of Poetry's relations to E. P.

    start with the beginning/ with what I sent to THEM and with the return made by them.

                        A minor stink in a very small kettle.

    and NO cause for me to have any pleasant recollection of any of Harriet's hams save Alice Corbin [Henderson] who was not a ham but did try to educate dear ole Harriet,

                    who was DUMB but honest,
and honesty is a form of intelligence.

I take it most cliques tend to pusillanimity

and if ole Jarge has at last
got on the band wagon, so much the better.

Racine will be good for Jarge. And Ronsard wont lead him into
any conflicts with the POLICE.

I am hoping to retain Va. residence, and as the brit tax lice will
dock 42½% of my britisch intake if I don't.

When a murkn displays the inDEEpendence of living outside the
jurisdiction of the Jewsfeld gestapo, the british minions soak him.

If you see any means of covering my air-transport hin and zuruk
some time in the autumn, hang onto it.

I shd/ enjoy some sallyOlunn
and a little purr-light conversation.

Sea air doing me good. Sad fer Mary
etc. that the mountain air didn't inflate my poumons. I gasped
like a whale out of water.

Please use present postal address till further warning.

I cert/ did NOT go to Paris to see the cigarette butts D'antan of
Miss Bleach's[7] KOlection.[8] But note with mild surprise that the
gestaunesc did not exclude my productions from it.

all of which is here writ acc/ the consteroeshun of Massachusetts
as inserted therein by J. Adams. i.e. with "good humor."

I got nawthing against old Jarge/ but Mr. Rago had better show
positive velleity.

Usually they reject what I send 'em[9]

Lot of meat in Stock's of the 17th, copy sent by him to Odlin
who shd/ remit to you.

Fuller JFC is in AGENDA No. 2. Maverick showed up here ten
days ago but doubt if he means to take violent action.

letter to L. C. Donnelly, returned marked "deceased"
which is a loss to the minority of honest men. A damn good
friend to E. P.

perhaps not very effective because he tried to push too many good ideas all at once.

shd/ be proper obit. printed somewhere.

I haven't Holden's address, or Pelly's and don't know who else knew enough about Donnerly to do it properly.

whether letter to either of 'em at L. C. D's old address wd. be forwarded

I dunno. it was

8203 Woodward Ave. Detroit 2, Mich.

undated review in Dutch paper (not labeled) by K. J. Hahn looks as if he had really got to relation of Rock-Drill to rest of poem.

Standpunkt, 12 July last year, also good notices, forwarded by Faber with usual celerity./

you might pass on this bib/n to G. Giovannini. along with enc. wop clip
interesting to see pore Archie accused of Oeezenstein's pewkerie

if so
he HAS wherefore to puppologize.

wot a narsty thing to have printed about one.

This is my postal address/ I hope to git a legal one in Arlington in time to fwustrate Weinstin Kirchbaum's trustees.

benedictions.

E. P. for which reason

trouble with *Poetry*/ it is useful as a trade paper. I bucked up Harriet to HAVE it continue when she was ready to stop. I also resigned repeatedly during 1st or 2nd/ year, but continued to try to keep some life in it.

BUT it has been run with total pusillanimity, eschewing all the vital life of the mind, all the things which make poetry worth writing and reading, all the indignations against the total decay

of civic life
and general slobbery.

and has fallen for freudian angle/ i.e. not what author gets onto
the page, but did he wet the bed as a child.

Pound was toying with the idea of selling some of W. C.
Williams' galleys and other items in his huge collection stored
in the basement at Schloss Brunnenburg, Merano. I had suggested that he write C. Waller Barrett, wealthy bibliophile
who had presented his collection of Americana, valued at
several millions of dollars, to The University of Virginia.
The poet passed the buck to me, but nothing came of this.
He worried about money, but Mrs. Pound assured me on
several occasions that although they didn't have enough to
live in luxury, or to travel, as in the old days, neither were
they in financial difficulties.

(41)

Hotel Italia, Rapallo

14 June (1959)

Thanks

Rather you deal with C. W. Barrett, as I am obviously non grata
in U. Va.

Galleys. W. C. W. Voyage to Pagany.[10]

1 Dialoghi del Bruno (i.e. Giordano Bruno)
   by A. Gozzi, with very interesting pencil notes
by Santayana, who gave me the book.

Cd. also do note on same, which wd. be the series of four, i.e.
Bruno, Gozzo, G. S. and y. v. t. but know no american periodicals
open to serious discussion even of innocuous matter

yrs

E. P.

(42)

17 Ap 59

H. M.

ONE sentence for verifax, not the rest of this note.
(LACK of local government is an effect, not a cause.)

end verifax.

you can send this and last installment to

Ralph Maupin 3030 Ramsey Ave. Dallas 16, Texas

and

Robt. Bly, "The Fifties" Brushwood Hill, Pine Island, Minn.

as well as
to LONG list #2

also to Dr. Jaime Garcia Terres,

Universidad Mexico, Mexico City, Mexico.

do write to Terres, expressing appreciation of his publication of
my 4 point program,[11] but asking WHAT paper it was in, and at
what date.

Am still interested in contacting Mrs. Cabell / please ask Bly if
his paper has continued.

NOTE Canto CI, in FINAL issue of European, and indicates high
quality of European for last and next to last issue.

and send Mensdorf installment Verifax

if yu pleez

also for verifax or quote in letters.

Wars are often caused by people who have strong ideas re/ the
conduct of others.

Dare say these two sentences better be put on sep/slip. but not
this letter for verifax.

Terres has fotorepred of my signed 4 points in english, but useful to see the spanish, and his excellent translation of poems as
display.

of/ Dagens Nyheter last Autumn.

I dont spose U. S. TV will use english, the BBC does occasionally use U. S. features.

I don't imagine the soi disant A. P. man has conveyed my message to 'em,

i.e. that if they don't use Pegler they can go to Hell.

(43)

HOTEL GRANDE ITALIA   RAPALLO

29 Maggio 59

DEAR H. M.

no Munich. may as well put Bridson[12] onto verifax.

add for FULL verifax (if not already there)

F. Grab   1717 A Parker St., Berkeley, Calif.

E. Mullins   2B 2239 Lincoln Ave. Chicago 14.

for this item and future

D. Gordon, Via Oleandri 37, Tirennia, (Pisa) Italy

Italian TV also sent something on sunday, but failed to notify me, as promised.

TRAXINIA sad/ to have gone well in Berlin.

DP sez add P. S.. "Yr/ shirt is invaluable."

for VERIFAX

E. P. Dissociates self from all movements which give excuse for distracting attention from SYSTEM of taxation,

issue of money included in that system.

every man has a right to have his ideas examined one at a time.

for full set verifax: Guy Davenport

340 Harvard St.   Apt 6
Cambridge   38 Mass.

H. M. might even subscribe to Gadfly for more life than in some
of the periodicals he seems to read. Ref/ Davenport.

    benedictions

E. P.

Pound had supplied two lists for photocopies, and D. G.
Bridson's name was on both, so when the letter was sent for
reproduction and distribution, a copy went to him. I have
Bridson's letter before me as I write, and it seems altogether
innocuous. He gives Pound a resume of the fourteen-minute
film as it went over the B.B.C., adding that the impact of the
poem, the setting (the film was made at the castle), and
Pound's personal performance was "really terrific." Bridson
had been a good friend to Pound and the poet did not want
to offend him. I can understand this, but I am at a loss to
explain why "Bridson was in agony."

The film Bridson made at Schloss Brunnenburg and used
in the broadcast was later distributed in America, and I had
it shown at the Richmond Public Library on Pound's
eightieth birthday. Excerpts of the interview were published
in *New Directions 17* (1961).

(44)

HOTEL ITALIA   17 June '59

DEAR H. M.

I suppose I never will learn. Thought verifax went only to
trusted few.

But Bridson in agony lest his letter shd get into hostile hands.

    Please ask everyone you sent it to to return their copies
if possible and not to mention existence of letter to anyone.

    Good will too valuable to jeopardize by my indiscretion.
And people already irritated by TV show ANYhow. What do
you know about the bugging of Mr. Long of La. the late huey's
brother.

This to explain telegram of this morning.

E. P.

(45)

HOTEL ITALIA
June 18 59

DEAR HARRY—

THANKS very much for comfort of telegram recd/ last evening. Br. "had copy anonymously and under impression that it was being supplied (?) by some group or organization."

which struck him as gross breach of confidence as done without consulting him.

which might well do him serious harm/ in fact he sees 30 years work to get where he COULD put over the "four steps" and

that program, go UP the flue,

and he never be able to be

associated with any further programmes of similar kind.

I was glad to get the good news from him, having wondered what he DID retain of the exhausting work at Brunnenburg that I sent it to you. being too weary and calcified to quote it properly and write to a dozen of the trusted.

ERROR entirely mine, but go ahead and recall it.

Am better, from being able to get a few sea baths / but can't stand altitude even

at Monte Allegro. just up funivia from here.

I wrote yesterday to Swabey, Cookson, Merchant, (no air mail to England from Italy) and by air to Grab, Horton, Giovannini, Miller, Odlin.

M/la says you might also have sent it to Del V /

can you let me know who else got it / am not sure my list of verifax/ is up to date.

                      or that all the dead wood has been cancelled from it.

BBC being now my main source of income, and ONLY outlet in England, any wear and tear on B/dn's nerves wd/ be MOST inconvenient and all my damn fault for being so

impeTUous and careless.

I will NEVER learn discretion.

Let's hope his signature is sufficiently illegible to conceal it even from the elect.

I ought to have recast the news/ and his address is on the verifax, and there is probably only one Goeffry in the BBC ANYhow. AND the s.o.b's are already gunning for him, as shows in ill tempered ref/ in Listener, (the BBC weakley). He has never been able to get the four steps PRINTED in england.

note from Bock (if you know who he is). Horton will.

Bock evidently been poking into ritual murder, kali worship, black magic, and the letter shows the extent of corruption raging in Washington. Not that he gives lucid account. BUT the letter shows.

Earl Long has made french news. Figaro printing his yell to reporters outside bughouse window. VURRY interesting.

have you any details? Wonder if Kilpatrick will notice some AMerican news routed to him from San Francisco VIA the Mediterranean.

Murkn Embassy has paid (that is to say pund sterling)

122/3/6

for permission to include some Ez in their Anthology of American Literature.

I don't know that they need to have paid it in furrin curency,

so that the britisch tax buggers get 42½%

of it. Or if there is any bright colleague

ready to animadvert on that highly amusing conwhatycallit

(unsigned)

(46)

HOTEL GRANDE ITALIA   RAPALLO

10 Lug. '59

H. M.

SHIRTS, and ye clothed me. philetelicly etc. than Q. If a guy named Colt asks you, do send him any verifax he wants. also send the lot to Gen. P. A. del Valle

9 Eastern Av. Annapolis Md.

AND as yu like to drive car, do GO in person and talk him into seeing Kerr.

The Jew Pork Herald Trib, Paris edn/ yowling about turn down of Strawsz, whom they spell Strauss.

which I take it is a damn good thing, but have no right to an opinion as I don't know enough about it.

Stinking anti-german puppygander still running in cinemas.

yrs briefly

EP

AND do send verifax Dagens Nyheter to Kilpatrick, from whom have had nice letter, saying I am above Richmond's head,

I have writ him a le'r in what I believe is clear and simple (as he requests) language. If he don't print it, try to git it fer verifax.

Early in 1959 the poet's health began deteriorating. In April Giovannini had word that Pound lacked energy, spent much time in bed, and had more than the usual trouble keeping his head up. This was diagnosed as low blood presure. Two months later he wrote that "calcification on 6th and other cerebral vertebrae slowing me down," adding, "it slows the mind as well as the body." His physical infirmities multiplied with the months, but the great brain gave ground grudgingly, for in the same letter to Giovannini he plans a new literary journal: "Can someone compile a list of those who want a periodical that can be consecutive at level of

Merchant in Yale Lit magazine? Do I need to send a list
of possible subscribers? . . . Has anyone even investigated
the personnel running official university periodicals like the
Virginia Quarterly, "New Mexico" the Farleigh Dickinson
apparently slanted, sent by Meacham. But has anyone looked
over the field for possible clean root anywhere?"

The poet rallied and seemed better for a few months, even
took Dorothy and Marcella on a short tour of Italy, returning,
of all places, to Pisa. No longer the caged panther of the
Pisan Cantos but a free man, a great man, whose pre-eminence
was acknowledged here in Dante country. But was it? In
July, 1959, Dr. Giovannini wrote me that a clipping from an
Italian newspaper reported that Eliot had been honored the
previous May by the city of Florence with a gold medal in
recognition of his work in propagating a knowledge of Dante
in the Anglo-Saxon world. Giovannini goes on to say he
deserves the honor for his 1929 booklet on Dante. But Eliot
is quoted as saying, in response to the citation presented by
the Italian Ambassador in London: "I don't consider myself
worthy of this high honor, but I willingly accept it because
I really could not name another who today would be more
worthy." Giovannini points out (all in good humor) that the
usually generous poet had a lapse of memory—if, he adds,
the quote is exact, for in the preface to that booklet by Eliot
he says, "I owe something to an essay by Mr. Ezra Pound
in his *Spirit of Romance*, but more to his table-talk." The
good Professor goes on to remind me of something we are
apt to forget, that Pound begins with Dante, that his first
book, *A Lume Spento*, takes its title from the *Purgatory*, and
that the essays in *Spirit of Romance* reveal that Pound went
to school in Dante's *De Vulgari Eloquentia*. But in this
Jamesian parenthesis my little book begins to take on the
coloring of a critique, which I am not qualified to write, in
place of the memoir I intend to record. In any case, T. S.

Eliot, a great, good friend of Pound's had much influence with the generation of poets beginning to write in the twenties and thirties, and he no doubt directed their attention to Dante. Pound was, and probably will remain, a poet's poet and will continue, so long as English is read, to influence the influential.

With *Thrones* in the hands of his publisher at last, the great poet found it increasingly difficult to concentrate on his major work (early in 1960 he told Donald Hall he was stuck), and he began to worry. He worried about his "failure" to achieve what he set out to do. As Mrs. Pound wrote me, "Ezra seems oppressed always by some sense of not having done what he should with his life. . . . it is depressing one can't boost him up on this." He was full of "regrets" for much he had said and done, and for much he hadn't done, and the press reported that at last Pound had seen the error of his ways, without commenting on his obvious loss of memory and his inability to concentrate. Pound, sorry? Not the Ezra Pound whose pronouncements, public and private, I had followed for fifty years.

In this mood, and before he went into his silence and ceased writing altogether, he wrote MacLeish and others in an un-Poundian tone of uncertainty and humility: "Forgive me for about 80% of the violent things I have said about some of your friends," he wrote "Archie," "some of them are deplorable, and it is too late to retract 'em. Violent language is an error. I did not get full of Agassiz. That would have saved me. . . ." In another note to MacLeish he says, "Wish you were in reach of conversation. A God-awful lot to get straightened out. For arrogance to my colleagues, etc., etc . . ." And later, "I got to Rome after a year [from the July, 1958 landing at Genoa] and collapsed, have been no use to myself . . ."

And he worried about money, needlessly, as it turned out,

although I didn't know this at the time. His situation was pretty much as it had always been. He had enough to live on and do some of the things he wanted to do but not enough to do all. Contributing to this anxiety was the fact that in furnishing and decorating an apartment in Rapallo he over-extended himself. He got into the hands of unscrupulous fellows, and it took the good offices of Prince Boris' father to straighten things out and get the prices reduced.

Knowing that his health was bad and his mind was failing I felt he should not have to worry about money. I believed every obstacle in the way of early completion of his *Cantos* should be removed. I felt one of the foundations would help but didn't know where to turn. Finally I wrote to a friend, C. Scott Fletcher, then President of the Fund for Adult Education. I knew Pound's situation would not come within the purview of their grants, but I knew "Scotty" would be sympathetic and helpful, and he was. He felt it unlikely that the larger foundations would do anything, and he suggested I try to locate several wealthy people who would be willing to put up the money, either from their personal funds or from a personal foundation. He knew that William Benton had expressed interest in Ezra and suggested that I write to him, since he had such a foundation. I found his reply so interesting I have included it.

ENCYCLOPAEDIA BRITANNICA
342 MADISON AVENUE
NEW YORK, N. Y.
December 29, 1959

DEAR MR. MEACHAM:

Your project is very appealing but it is not for me. My Foundation operates wholly in the field of communications. Now I agree that Mr. Ezra Pound is himself a great monument to the art of communicating. My goals are different, and much lower. I am sorry. Most worthy and exciting appeals come to me weekly. If I

allowed my resources to be dissipated I would be ineffective. I
hope you will understand. And I do congratulate you for your
leadership.

WILLIAM BENTON

Publisher and Chairman

In answer to my inquiry, Mrs. Pound wrote that while a
grant might cheer Ezra up he was getting royalties and she
had some money in her own name. Yet she said he worried
"about not earning." In closing she said the poet was not well
enough to do any writing, and was having some injections.
"Years in an asylum," she observed wryly, "don't do one any
good if one *isn't* crazy!" In any event, nothing came of this,
although I wrote to half a dozen "floundations" (as Ezra
called them) and was also in touch with Norman Holmes
Pearson and Donald Hall.

(47)

1 Jan '60

DEAR MEACHAM

Thanks for magnificent red corduroy shirt and everything.
Sorry you are ill. Best for 1960 and to the ladies.

I get stupider and stupider and fail to keep up with my correspondence, as you know better than anyone else.

Young poets keep getting brighter and brighter, often in Cummings' and Marianne's feathers. BUT writing better and brighter
and so forth.

Francis Nielson is said to be 94, wonder do you know of him. I
have seen the outside of some of his books, but haven't the guts
to dig into 'em.

Stuff published by C. C. Nelson, Appleton, Wis,
(Nielson is the mans name, Nelson is the co.)

Let me end this before I get distracted again.

Note that there are various drafts of Cantos, after 109.

Also parts cut from the Thrones.

                              Some may be worth saving.

dont overwork yourself and etc. etc. don't worry your new boss
with that Mimeograph.

                                                      EP

The following two letters were written from Rome when
the poet was having a bad spell. He refers to the possibility
of a grant and expresses the hope that he may get to Edin-
burgh. Noel Stock was renting one of the apartments in the
castle and had been given access to the priceless papers
stored in the castle with the understanding that he would
bring some order out of the chaos there. He seems, instead,
to have spent most of his time gathering material for several
books about Pound and his work. He came to the poet
through their mutual interest in Social Credit, and they corresponded for years. After editing a small magazine, *Edge*,
in Australia, he made the pilgrimage to Merano; then came
the disillusionment. He criticized Pound's interpretation of
economic and historical data and, on the whole, condemned
the plan and the poetry of the *Cantos*.[13] In any case, he
seems to have gotten into the poet's hair, and he wanted to
get rid of him.

The second letter from Rome, dated February 8, 1960
reflects a remarkable, if temporary, upswing. The "brief
spurt of energy" was brief indeed.

                              (48)

co U Dadone   ROMA, ITALY

                                              (*undated*)

DEAR HM.

Yes of course I'd dump any amount of blessing on you. but
if there is any money [torn] [wouldn't] it be (very *ill* and tired)
if you get any $ can discuss how to apply 'em, possibly more
likely to pay my expenses to Edinburg IF [Sacher] gets Trexinia

into Festival—on chance of getting it done RIGHT. choric dances—
dea ex machina *masks*, especially Herakles metamorphoses, can
you get Stock a job in U. S. A. to cover his food and back rent,
& not have him in danger of starving in Brunnenburg basement—
ever

E. P.

or his fragments

(49)

co/ U.Dadone

80 VIA ANGELOPOLIZIANO, ROMA, ITALY

8 Feb (1960)

DEAR H. M.

having been lent this perfect typewriter by practical journalist.
No idea who or what S/ is. in yrs of whatever brief note.

Hope to contact Hall

Brief spurt of energy, thought wd be useful to open up Richmond
News Leader. long let lie without busting into. wd be useful for
reduced railway fare IF I ever get mobilized.

I don't suppose Richmond cares a hoot re/ Italian reaction to
Gronchi's visit to Moscow.

Have you any idea what Kilpatrick does print re Europe.
American kulchur of the marx bros/ about to invade these shores
and Disney Lands.

Haven't carbons here but on reflection if S/ needs a job he needs
a job. I mean if he is the S/ you refer to crypticly [Noel Stock].

Whoever S/is, I introduced the topic I was serious. Amn't I
always serious, too serious?

(*unsigned*)

Donald Hall, who occupies a place in the front rank of
contemporary American poets, has been my friend since he
read for The Poetry Society of Virginia when he was in his
twenties. He had won the Oxford Newdigate Prize, and his

first volume of poems was the Lamont Poetry Selection of
The Academy of American Poets. At the time of this correspondence he was Poetry Editor of *The Paris Review* and a
member of the English Department at The University of
Michigan. Don had made an unsuccessful attempt to interview Pound at St. Elizabeths, and he wanted to try again.
Since there was no more prestigious literary journal in
America than *The Paris Review*, I was all for it. Don
would spend a year's leave in England, and we conspired to
bring about the interview.

I wrote Ezra that in my opinion Don was the best of
the young advancing poets, adding, "He would like very
much to do a 'straight *Paris Review* interview—not one on
criticism, but on Pound, Poetry, and his opinions.' He interviewed Eliot for the March issue and now he wants to go
after big game! He has asked me if I would mention this to
you and see if you will see him. Hall closed his letter to me,
'You must know how much I admire that man. He's taught
me more than anybody has'."

Meanwhile, I was still trying to raise money for Pound
and had asked Norman Holmes Pearson to accept the chair-
manship of the fund, if we could get one going. So I asked
Don to sound the poet out on it. Ezra would accept the
fellowship or whatever, Don wrote, but he was not enthu-
siastic; he wanted to *earn*. Nothing came of this effort, but
the interview was a huge success. Dorothy wrote: "Don
Hall has seen Ezra in Rome, and E. evidently likes him,
writing that Hall is 'zestful' for which thank heaven!" After
he returned to England Don wrote that Pound wanted to
live in the United States but would settle for a three-month
lecture tour.

Don wrote, ". . . As a man I found him extremely thoughtful and warm and generous. I saw no paranoia. I saw nothing
insane, only a sort of aphasiac losing of the thread of memory.
He hasn't written since July [1959]. The last day I was there

he showed me the notes and drafts of the next five cantos, and they appeared to me to include some of the best stuff anywhere, really fine, with the exaltation he needs in the Paradiso . . ."

(50)

BRUNNENBURG TIROLO, MERANO ITALY

11 Aug 1960

DEAR MEACHAM

I ought to be fried in oil for not answering yr/ letters, and for not having sent thanks that you have been getting thru yr/ operation

etc. and saluti,

but the plain fact is that my head just doesn't WORK. Stretches when it just doesn't work.

Hall has done pretty well by me.

saluti to Madame M/

E. P.

The following letter was in answer to my note of March 11, 1960, in which I asked if Charles Norman's biography, which was to be published in the fall, was authorized.

(51)

(undated)

DEAR MEACHAM

No, the Norman is not authorized but it will look dangerously like it.

Lot of eulogy, in the samples sent

but. . . . . heaven knows what else is there?

He did a book on cummings, to which I contributed a lot of pro cummings stuff free.

Have been trying to write you for weeks.

Hall a great comfort, but I don't know how far he can get.

                                                      E. P.

The following handwritten note came shortly after I had
undergone major surgery that led to my retirement:

                         (52)

      DEAR HARRY

                    Tank god
                 you are
                     coming thru
                     yr operation
                              E

                       (7/60)

The mind that had purified the language of the tribe and
the body that had withstood the rigors of the "gorilla cage"
at Pisa, and the madhouse in Washington, now declined
steadily, and in 1960 the poet went into his silence. At about
the same time, he developed a urinary infection while in
Rome and spent three weeks in a clinic there. Dorothy
reported that he returned to Rapallo "the middle of June,
and was deposited at the Rest House just outside the city.
Mary and I go down alternate days to visit him." She went
on to say he was very weak and was confined to his bed,
ate little, and was again troubled with low blood pressure.
She added, "He looks very handsome and white." From that
time on he was up and down and in the summer of 1962
underwent surgery for prostate infection. The following
May he had a second operation in the clinic at Rapallo,
performed by a surgeon from Genoa. Afterward, he seemed
to grow stronger, but he rarely spoke and seems to have
quit writing altogether. Few, I think, would challenge Mrs.
Pound's reason for this silence: "Too much terrible anxiety
loaded onto such a sensitivity."

    And so the pattern of the poet's life changed again. No

more controversies. "No more to sing and scold by the Latin sea," but old in mind and body, and thinking God knows what thoughts, he followed the sun from the Alps to Rome, to Venice (which he loved more than any city, next to Rapallo) and then, in the winter to Sant' Ambrogia where he could sit and gaze upon the loudsounding sea. Honors came to him. In 1962 *Poetry* gave him the Harriet Monroe Memorial Prize, and in 1963 he was awarded the $5,000 Fellowship of the Academy of American Poets. Scholars from all over the world came to see him and were met with silence. Twice he attended Gian Carlo Menotti's Festival of Two Worlds at Spoleto, Italy. In July 1965 his opera, *The Testament of François Villon,* was performed as a ballet, but he seems to have considered it "a waste of time." As Dorothy pointed out to me, "It was written to be sung in French always; the music for each song was especially fitted word for word." At the 1966 Festival he was introduced by Patrick Creagh, English poet, as "the most important single factor in modern English-language poetry," and he read, briefly, from "Hugh Selwyn Mauberley," "Canto XIII," and "some work in progress." As Robert C. Doty reported the occasion for the *New York Times* of July 18, 1966, "His voice was weak, tremulous and almost inaudible at first, but the poet gained strength and confidence as he went on. . . ."

Although not strong enough for the trip, Pound flew to London in February 1965 to attend memorial services for his late, great friend, T. S. Eliot, held at Westminster Abbey. He also called on Mrs. Eliot, who wrote me, "I did indeed have a most moving visit from Ezra Pound when he came to London for my husband's memorial service. It meant much to me to welcome him to our home." Pound mentions this obliquely in a tribute he wrote for the memorial edition of the *Sewanee Review.*[14] "I had hoped to see him in Venice this year for the Dante Commemoration at the Giorgio Cini Foundation—instead: Westminster Abbey. But, later, on his own hearth, a flame tended, a presence felt." Since Dublin —and the entire world, for that matter—was celebrating William Butler Yeats Centennial, Pound and the companion who was caring for him (Dorothy was not equal to the trip) flew to Ireland for a visit with Yeats's widow. In writing to me about this leg of the journey Dorothy said, "She [Mrs. Yeats] was a great friend of mine. As girls we went sketching together in the holidays."

On October 30, 1965 the poet was eighty years old, and he was honored in many ways. L'Herne of Paris made plans for the publication of what they hoped would be the definitive French edition of his works, and the publisher gave Pound a trip to Athens for a birthday present. A number of commemorative books appeared, including Stock's *Ezra Pound, Perspectives*.[15] Magazines here and abroad ran Pound issues and articles. *Agenda*, a literary journal published in London and edited by William Cookson, was perhaps the most representative, for it contained tributes by such poets and scholars as Robert Lowell, Marianne Moore, Basil Bunting, Hugh Kenner, and John Berryman. Columbia Broadcasting System's *Camera Three* presented a three-part series written by Stephan Chodorov entitled *In Search of Ezra Pound*. But the Mover and Shaker was silent.

While I still send Ezra birthday greetings and Christmas cards, our correspondence ended with the following notes.

(53)

3 Nov 1960

DEAR AND GENEROUS MEACHAM

My grititude for all you have done, I wish you hadn't had so much trouble with your insides. I've been a poor correspondent. God send you some tranquility. And the strength to enjoy it.

15 Dec. and that was writ 3 weeks ago. I dodder and dont get the letters written. God bless you, Meacham, and give you the best there is to be had. And salute Mrs. Meacham for me.

E. P.

(54)

(undated)

DEAR MEACHAM

cold as hen's teeth here in this mountain, and on 3rd **Nov I** started to write to you, and commiserate your physical troubles, and thank you for the friendship.

God bless you for all you have done, and forgive me my **con**-tinuous muddle and bless Mrs. Meacham

E. P.

Appendix

Letters from George Dillon, Richard Wilbur, Hugh Kenner, G. Giovannini, and others should be published, and no doubt they will be some day, for I have presented my papers to the Alderman Library of The University of Virginia. The following are included as typical of the correspondence on the Pound case.

342 Buena Vista Road   Sante Fe, N.M.

Jan 13, 1958

The Honorable Herbert Brownell
The Attorney General
Washington, D. C.

Dear Mr. Brownell:

Understanding that there are steps again toward the release of Ezra Pound from detention in St. Elizabeths Hospital, I should like to put in my word urging such action.

Having known Ezra nearly fifty years, I realize that certain of his aspects might not seem normal to the ordinary observer but I have never thought him any less balanced than William Blake and have felt that outside his odd balance he might not have been similarly gifted.

Since I have never heard the broadcasts which occasioned the difficulties with our government, I cannot judge as to the charges of treason but I feel certain that he was only continuing his characteristic and, it would seem to me, harmless outbursts against whatever authorities and beliefs that be. And I am also certain that his actions outside of St. Elizabeths would not be seriously prejudicial to the safety of society.

In other words, I heartily join with other citizens in hoping that he may be, after these years, set free.

Very truly yours,

Witter Bynner

195

Mr. Brooks had written *Esquire* commending the Pound article the magazine ran in late 1957. I added his name to my list and he sent the following card.

VAN WYCK BROOKS   BRIDGEWATER   CONNECTICUT

Oct. 4, 1957

DEAR MR. MEACHAM,

Thank you for your letter. I have written to the Attorney General in Washington urging the release of Ezra Pound.

Yours sincerely,

VAN WYCK BROOKS

BAREN (N. H.) HOLLAND VAN NISPENSTRAAT 39

17 December '57

DEAR MR. MEACHAM:

I am happy to add my letter to others addressed to the Attorney General asking for a review of Mr. Pound's case with a view toward his release from St. Elizabeths. My letter to the AG goes off today.

Whatever his wrongheadedness in other matters, Mr. Pound's poetic intelligence, as Allen Tate pointed out so well many years ago, is of the finest, and, if he doesn't always know what substantively he is talking about, he does know poetry and how to write it.

It is a good cause in which you are working. If released, I hope Mr. Pound will be allowed to live in freedom, without being badgered by committees of any kind which may feel it their duty to investigate him farther. His sins are clearly on his head and written plainly in the record for any one to read, and, if health is still with him, he will inevitably find other words to say. Some of them, I am sure, will be angry and unintentionally vindicative, others may reach again toward poetry. And that will be good for him and for us.

Whether he writes again or not, or whatever the ultimate judgment on the justice of his incarceration, it will be good for us and for the people who care for poetry who come after us to know that our finest poetic voice was allowed final freedom.

Yours very sincerely,

LEWIS LEARY

(SEAL OF THE U. N.)

SECRETARY-GENERAL   23 November 1957

DEAR MR. MEACHAM,

I thank you for your letter of 18 October. My reply has been delayed because I had hoped for some further information before telling you about my views on the question you raised.

I am indeed most interested in securing Mr. Pound's release. I have done what I could to further a possible solution. However, I am insufficiently informed about the results of my efforts so far to say anything about them.

What I have tried to do has been linked with the efforts of others concerning which I may perhaps refer you to Professor Archibald MacLeish at Harvard with whom you undoubtedly have been in touch already.

I agree with you that any publicity at this time would be ruinous and our exchange of views will be kept on a strictly confidential basis by me as I trust by you.

I would appreciate any information you might care to give me about further developments. If you see any point on which I might be helpful, I am sure you will inform me.

Sincerely,

DAG HAMMARSKJÖLD

As the poet points out, he has never published the Newark poem, but it did appear in print under unusual and, I think, amusing circumstances. In 1915 the Newark Poetry Competition was announced as part of the celebration of the 250th anniversary celebration of the founding of the city in 1666. The judges were the mayor, the head of the English Department in a local high school, the associate editor of a

Newark newspaper, a professor of the history of art, the literary editor of a national humor magazine, a judge of the Circuit Court, and a little-known writer of verses.

The winning poems, as well as the runners-up, were published by the Committee of One Hundred under the title, *The Newark Anniversary Poems* (Laurence J. Gomme, New York). Prizes totaling $1,000 were distributed as follows: Clement Wood, $250, Anna Blake Mezquida, $150, and Albert E. Trombly, $100. Pound's poem appears in ninth place among ten which were awarded $50 each.

In a chapter titled "The Sunny Side" the author, presumably Henry Wellington Wack, comments on some of the poets and has a word or two to say about the current situation of poetry; current, that is, fifty years ago. "That philosophic iconoclast, Ezra Pound, earlier exponent of the Imagist School of Poetic Palpitation writing from London, assaulted our civic sensibilities in a poem of violence directed at the head, heart, and hands of Newark. Of his poem, one of the judges remarked that it is 'Captious, arrogant, hypercritical, but some merit.' Another judge cast it into the discard. Also there is food for thought in our London poet's catechistic cadences." In summing up, the editor wrote: "The intellectuals; the cognoscenti; the Dolly Dinkles of the cubistic literature; the weird profundities of the Imagists; interpreting the scrap heap of mad emotions; all have joined the obscurantists of the obvious and serenaded the heights and the abyss with their tatterdemalion poetry. Let us not begrudge him the high appraisal of our poetry judges."

Mrs. Pound agrees that the poem, with its "catechistic cadences" ought to be reprinted and included in the Pound canon.

TO A CITY SENDING HIM ADVERTISEMENTS

BUT will you do all these things?
　You, with your promises,
　You, with your claims to life,
Will you see fine things perish?
Will you always take sides with the heavy;
Will you, having got the songs you ask for,
　Choose only the worst, the coarsest?
Will you choose flattering tongues?

Sforza . . . Baglione!
Tyrants, were flattered by one renaissance,
　And will your Demos,
Trying to match the rest, do as the rest,
The hurrying other cities,
Careless of all that's quiet,
Seeing the flare, the glitter only?

Will you let quiet men
　　　live and continue among you,
　Making, this one, a fane,
　This one a building;
Or this bedevilled, casual, sluggish fellow
Do, once in a life, the single perfect poem,
　And let him go unstoned?
Are you alone? Others may talk
　　　and chatter about their promises,
Others have fooled me when I sought the soul.
And your white slender neighbor,
　　　a queen of cities,
A queen ignorant, can you outstrip her;
　Can you be, say,
　As Pavia's Pavia
And not Milan swelling and being modern
　　　despite her enormous treasure?

If each Italian city is herself,
　Each with a form, light, character,

To love and hate one, and be loved and hated,
    never a blank, a wall, a nullity;
Can you, Newark, be thus,
    setting a fashion
But little known in our land?
    The rhetoricians
Will tell you as much. Can you achieve it?
You ask for immortality, you offer a prize for it,
    a price, a prize, and honour?
You ask a life, a life's skill,
    bent to the shackle,
    bent to implant a soul
    in your tick commerce?
    Or the God's foot
    struck on your shoulder
    effortless,
    being invoked, properly called,
    invited?
I throw down his ten words,
    and we are immortal?

In all your hundreds of thousands
    who will know this;
Who will see the God's foot,
    who catch the glitter,
The silvery heel of Apollo;
    who know the oblation
Accepted, heard in the lasting realm?

If your professors, mayors, judges . . .?
    Reader, we think not . . .
Some more loud-mouthed fellow,
    slamming a bigger drum,
Some fellow rhyming and roaring,
    Some more obsequious hack,
Will receive their purple,
    be the town's bard,
Be ten days hailed as immortal,
    But you will die or live
    By the silvery heel of Apollo.

Prayers

In May 1953, and no doubt for years prior to that time, the girls in Sister Therese's class in versification at Trinity College, Washington, D. C., had prayed for Pound's release. Giovannini told the poet about it and, he replied, "Gratitude to the sisters/ what about directing the prayer more specifically / focus on intrigue and the needed LIGHT." The scholar sent a copy of the letter, which he says reads like one of the cantos, along with a gloss (example: "Light" which connects with Neo-platonic, Dantean light of the *Cantos*). His friend had sent the poet passages from Keats's letters on Milton, attacking *Paradise Lost as* "a corruption of our language." Since Pound had a pretty low opinion of Milton he was delighted: "Waaal/ Johnnie Keats has that ONE UP / better print it."

Usura

Pound has said many times, in and out of print (like all men who talk a great deal and have a great deal to say, he repeats himself, but he is *never* dull) that the *Usura Cantos* would not be difficult if one knew the meaning of the word usury. It is not, he says, to be confused with legitimate interest due, teleologically, to the increase in domestic animals and plants. *Usura* is a charge for the use of purchasing power levied without regard to production, often without regard even to the possibilities of production.

Anti-Semitism

Pound's peculiar form of intellectual anti-Semitism (if it *is* anti-Semitism) is a puzzlement. As James Kilpatrick said in his article quoted in full here, "I venture the positive assertion that Pound's anti-Semitism never will inspire the faintest urge in anyone to put a torch to a synagogue. . . ."

In a letter to Giovannini (November 10, 1957) he added the following postscript,

denial by or even TO some notable re/ some of the worst and MOST repeated lies might be useful. as to race hatred/ as to disease of THOUGHT. battaglia ideologica, is not necessarily excitement to pogrom.

Confucian angle same for jew as for anyone else/ IF a man is a Jew, let him develop his racial virtues, not his racial vices.

same for a damnbrit/ or a frog-wop.

in my voluminous anterior scribbles

Must be paragraphs somewhere re/ the racial anti-type

i.e. the guy who notices defects of his race or environment and tries to produce antidote.

He wrote MacLeish on June 17, 1956 (and the statement is in print somewhere) ". . . Ez considers anti-Semitism un-Aristotelian and unscientific."

Silence and Remorse?

It is a source of irritation to me, and, I have every reason to believe, to Mrs. Pound also, that there is so much pussyfooting and distortion about the perfectly obvious fact that Pound's great mind has been failing since his illness in 1960. It is remarkable that he ever recovered his wits after confinement in the "gorilla cage" at Pisa and after months with the criminally insane at St. Elizabeths when his life was always in danger, before he was moved to Chestnut Ward. That he *did* recover after his breakdown at Pisa, the large body of his work, begun at the Disciplinary Training Center, stands as eloquent testimony. (Since reports of the length of Pound's confinement vary widely, it might be well to point out that he was held for thirteen years and thirteen days. He was taken into custody on May 5, 1945 and released on April 18, 1958. He was brought to Washington in November 1945.

He spent some time in the District of Columbia jail and was held briefly at Gallinger Hospital. He was confined at St. Elizabeths for twelve years and two months.)

His enemies would have him on his knees begging forgiveness for God knows what crimes; well-meaning friends, who should know better, would picture this giant, shorn of his strength, as an apologetic old man who wants to make his peace with the world. I included the last two letters he wrote to me for no other purpose than to show that he was not the poet who wrote the *Pisan Cantos* or *Thrones*. Since Mrs. Pound did not object, I assume she agrees with me. In fact, she has written that she does not accept his "regrets."

The November 5, 1965 issue of *Time* quotes the poet as having told his French publisher, Dominique de Roux, "I did not enter the silence. Silence captured me." The publisher explained that the silence indicates "a profound sense of remorse." This is a matter of opinion, and I doubt that M. Dominique de Roux is qualified to have an expert opinion on this subject.

Two years earlier, Grazia Livi, who interviewed the poet for the March, 1963 issue of *Epoca*, published in Venice, approached the poet with sympathy, understanding, and profound admiration. He saw Pound as one "sinking beyond the illusory borders of the world. He is not any more a man, but a symbol, who keeps only formal rapport with life; not a personage, but a presence who looks at the vicissitudes of this world with a soul completely freed, already far away, already thinking in the tragic and illuminated wisdom which precedes the end." Addressing the poet, he said, "Everybody speaks of Pound as a very remote figure . . . so I was almost afraid of coming to you." And the poet replied, "Afraid? I understand . . . everything I touch I ruin." And again, "I don't think, I have only the certitude of my incertitude."

Notes

Part One

1. *T.P.'s Weekly* was published by T. P. O'Connor, popular journalist-personality of the era. Founded in 1902, it merged with *Today* in 1916, and in 1923 resumed the old name. It discontinued publication in 1929.

2. Mr. Donald E. Thompson, Librarian, Lilly Library, Wabash College, wrote me on March 30, 1967, "I am enclosing an article from the *Wabash Bulletin*, December 1963, written by R. E. Banta. In preparing the article Mr. Banta used all the sources we have including the faculty and trustee minutes. . . . I have not been able to locate in our college any information on the accusations. The article by Mr. Banta, "Ezra Pound Among the Hoosiers," points out that certain courses in the Department of Romance Languages had been abandoned, and the students requested permission to substitute other credits for work begun in French Language and Literature. "Sure enough, when the annual catalog, *sine qua non* of all official college action, appeared in April 1908, it listed Ezra Loomis Pound among the faculty but his name was marked by an asterisk. That, in turn, referred to another asterisk followed by the word 'Resigned.'" The student magazine, *The Wabash,* carried several references to Pound's absence from chapel, and the March 1908 issue "carried a further clue inserted among fillers of humorous intent . . . its substance is clear; Professor Pound had not left the institution entirely of his own volition:

> There are many cantankerous tumors,
> But none so noisesome as rumours,
> The Powers they said 'Zounds!'
> We'll have to can Pounds,
> He's going too far with the roomers!"

It is certain that Pound and Wabash were not meant for each other, and this is no reflection on either. On April 11, 1967, Mr. Banta wrote me that "If the college permitted itself to lose Pound my guess is that the college was right—and not only on account of the foolish episode of the burlesque lady. My guess is that Pres. Mackintosh handed Pound an extra $100 as an inducement to go elsewhere."

3. Although the term "Vorticism" is usually applied to the visual arts, it is related directly to modern poetry through Pound's interest in it, and his claim for it as a movement parallel to Imagism.

4. *Letters of Ezra Pound,* edited by D. D. Paige, Harcourt, Brace & Company, New York, 1950.

5. Giovannini informs me that this is a slight misquotation from *Inferno* IV. It reads "Among the masters of those who know." It should be *"Vidi il maestro di color che sanno,"* "I saw the master of those who know," the

master being Aristotle and the speaker the poet who is the guest of Virgil in the castle in Limbo.

6. Once on the lawn at St. Elizabeths, when Pound and Giovannini were discussing the poet's return to the Rome Radio after Pearl Harbor, he told his friend, *sotto voce,* "Perhaps I was a bit foolish."

7. T. S. Eliot, *Poetry* magazine, September 1946.

8. Dorothy Pound wrote me on March 31, 1967: "Riccardo degli Uberti, son of Ezra's great friend Admiral Ubaldo degli Uberti, was head of the Black Shirts in Germany when war broke. Now with publishing house in Florence." Their ancestor, Farinata degli Uberti, was one of the heretics Dante puts in hell (*Inferno* X). Pound refers to Farinata and Ubaldi in "Canto LXVIII."

9. *The Medical, Legal, Literary and Political Status of Ezra (Loomis) Weston Pound* . . . Congressional Record Appendix A3894, Tuesday, April 29, 1958. Like a great many who wrote about the case, Mr. Seiber mistakenly assumed that Robert Frost acted independently, for he adds, as a note: "Apparently Mr. Frost began individual lobbying for Mr. Pound's release during 1957, after earlier attempts by Archibald MacLeish and Mr. Frost and an English Committee had failed."

10. Eustice Mullins, *This Difficult Individual, Ezra Pound.* Fleet Publishing Company. Charles Norman, *Ezra Pound,* Macmillan Company.

11. Probably members of the Communist underground, or Partigiani.

12. Mary de Rachewiltz, *Ezra Pound at Eighty.* Esquire, April 1966.

13. Ezra Pound, *The Pisan Cantos.* New Directions, 1948.

14. *Ibid.* (LXXXIII).

Part Two

1. *Poetry.* September, 1946.

2. The letter also contains the following: "It has always been a good feeling for me that I brought about through Small, Maynard & Company his first publication in this country."

3. *New Masses,* in its Christmas 1945 issue asked rhetorically, in a cover headline, "Should Ezra Pound be Shot?"

4. House Resolution No. 403, introduced by Congressman Burdick, of North Dakota, on August 21, 1957:

WHEREAS Ezra Pound has been incarcerated in Saint Elizabeths Hospital for the past twelve years on the assumption that he is insane; and

WHEREAS, many people visit him there and are convinced that he is not insane: Therefore be it

Resolved, That the Committee on the Judiciary, acting as a whole or by subcommittee, is authorized and directed to conduct a full and complete investigation and study of the sanity of Ezra Pound, in order to determine whether there is justification for his continued incarceration in Saint Elizabeths Hospital . . .

The resolution lays down the rules under which the committee or subcommittee shall function, and then requires that "The committee shall report to the House on or before the first day of the second session of the present [85th] Congress the results of its investigation and study, together with such recommendations as it deems advisable."

5. Major General John Frederick Charles Fuller, C.B.C.B.E., served in the British Army in World War I. He is the author of more than a dozen books, including, *The Decisive Battles of the Western World and Their Influence upon History.*

6. Admiral Sir Barry Domvile, K.B.E., served with distinction in World War I, was later President of the Royal Naval College and Director of the Naval Intelligence Division. He retired from His Majesty's Navy in 1936.

7. Lieutenant General P. A. del Valle, U.S.M.C. (Retired), was, at the time of this correspondence, president of Defenders of the American Constitution, Inc.

8. The things Pound says should be tax deductible are in fact so. He evidently did not know United States tax practice.

9. The city was Newark, New Jersey, not Trenton.

10. The poem is reprinted in the Appendix.

11. Italian confections I had sent from Richmond.

12. Philip Marston, Boston Public Latin School.

13. J. Lindsay Almond, then Governor of Virginia.

14. Dr. Joseph Francis Rock, anthropologist, died in 1965. His work on the Na-Khi, their customs and myths, came into Pound's hands through a friend.

15. Peter Goullart was a friend of Rock's and dedicated to him a beautifully written book on the Na-Khi, *Forgotten Kingdom,* John Murray: London, 1955. He escaped with his mother from Russia during the revolution. Pound liked his book and entertained him at the castle in Merano.

16. Ezra Pound, *Guide to Kulchur.* New Directions, Norfolk, Connecticut, 1938.

17. Dudley Fitts, *New York Times Book Review,* July 3, 1960. Along the same line Hugh Kenner, in "Ezra Pound and Money" (*Agenda,* October-November, 1965) quotes Pound as saying, "People often think me crazy when I make a jump instead of a step, just as if all jumps were unsound and never carried one anywhere."

18. *Letters of Ezra Pound,* edited by D. D. Paige. Harcourt, Brace and Company, New York, 1950.

19. Ezra Pound, *Guide to Kulchur.* New Directions, Norfolk, Connecticut, 1938.

20. *Letters of Ezra Pound,* edited by D. D. Paige. Harcourt, Brace and Company, New York, 1950.

21. *Literary Essays of Ezra Pound.* New Directions, Norfolk, Connecticut, 1954. As used by Pound *melopoeia* means words charged with some musical property in addition to the ordinary meaning but has some bearing on it.

22. *ABC of Reading.* New Directions, New York, 1960. First published in 1934.

23. *Literary Essays of Ezra Pound.* New Directions, New York, 1954.

24. Harcourt, Brace & World, New York, 1965.

25. Holt, Rinehart & Winston, New York, 1966.

26. Thurman Arnold, *Fair Fights and Foul*. Harcourt, Brace & World, New York, 1965, and Julien Cornell's *The Trial of Ezra Pound*. John Day Company, New York, 1966.

27. Holt, Rinehart & Winston, New York, 1964.

28. Inserted in the *Congressional Record* by Congressman Burdick, May 6, 1958.

29. Dr. Marion R. King, then Head Psychiatrist of the United States Public Health Service, and one of the four psychiatrists who examined Pound on orders from the court.

30. The question of whether Pound was nominated for the Nobel Prize cannot now be resolved. After I had seen Mr. MacLeish's letter I wrote Bo Hammarskjöld, brother of the late Dag Hammarskjöld, to see what light he could shed on the question, and he answered, in part: "I am sorry to say that I know nothing at all about the questions put to me in your last letter. In fact, as a general rule, the recommendations for the Nobel Prize in Literature are to be held secret by the Royal Swedish Academy, its members and officials. But nominations can be made from many other sources, here and abroad, so it is possible that Mr. Pound can have been nominated from elsewhere. But I don't think that it will be possible for you or somebody else to get to know that from official sources. It follows that as far as I know there is nothing in the public records about a nomination of Mr. Pound." But the story did get into the newspapers here and in Europe. Giovannini said that while he has lost the clipping there was an Associated Press report that two Americans were nominees for the prize, but Pound was not mentioned. When he showed this to Pound, the poet, in turn, showed him a European magazine in which it was reported that three writers had been nominated, Pound among them.

31. On February 20, 1949 the Library of Congress announced that the first annual award of the Bollingen Prize in Poetry had been made to Ezra Pound for his book, the *Pisan Cantos*. This was done on the basis of a recommendation by a jury of selection consisting of the Fellows in American Letters of the Library of Congress. This group, appointed by the Librarian of Congress, consisted of the following writers: Conrad Aiken, W. H. Auden, Louise Bogan, Katherine Garrison Chapin, T. S. Eliot, Paul Green, Robert Lowell, Katherine Anne Porter, Karl Shapiro, Allen Tate, Willard Thorp, and Robert Penn Warren. Léonie Adams, the Library's Consultant in Poetry, also served on this jury. The award set off one of the bitterest literary controversies of the century.

32. The National Institute of Arts and Letters was founded in 1898 to foster excellence in literature and the fine arts in the United States. About two hundred and fifty Americans compose its membership. Fifty of these are elected to the American Academy of Arts and Letters, the National Institute's guiding body. Pound was elected a member of the National Institute in 1938. On the evening of May 25, 1958 Giovannini was visiting Pound and La Drière in the latter's apartment. While his two friends were conversing the poet was going over a copy of the proceedings of the Institute. He was humming and groaning, jumping up and walking around, and in every way possible showing his displeasure over the way the organization was being run. Finally, he sat down to type his letter of resignation. Alarmed at this sudden turn of events, his friends tried to persuade him to destroy

it, pointing out that he could best change things from within the organization. But he was adamant. Giovannini and La Drière adjourned to the kitchen to marshal their forces, and when they returned Pound had disappeared. He had gone to post the letter. Miss Felicia Geffen, Assistant to the President of The American Academy of Arts and Letters, has been kind enough to confirm receipt of this letter, adding, "however, his name was not removed from the membership list until 1960."

33. Wife of the poet Theodore Morrison, who was at that time director of the Bread Loaf Writers' Conference. Both helped Frost through the difficult period following his wife's death, and Mrs. Morrison stayed on as a sort of executive secretary.

34. *Selected Letters of Robert Frost*, edited by Lawrance Thompson. Holt, Rinehart & Winston, New York, 1964.

35. Ernest Hemingway.

36. T. S. Eliot.

37. Thurman Arnold, *Fair Fights and Foul*. Harcourt, Brace & World, New York, 1965.

Part Three

1. *National Review*. New York, May 24, 1958.

2. This is the essence but the details are more dramatic. As Pound was introduced to the editor and the reporter he said, with a twinkle in his eyes, "Gentlemen, remember the newspaperman's first commandment: thou shalt not commit accuracy."

3. Julien Cornell, *The Trial of Ezra Pound*. The John Day Company, New York, 1966. The title of this book raises an interesting question, and while I have no intention of exploring it, one should bear in mind that the record shows Pound was never tried. Perhaps Mr. Cornell is using layman's language, or he may be suggesting trial by the press.

4. Early in 1966 the papers were transferred from the damp basement of the castle to Yale University. As yet (May, 1967) there has been no sale or legal conveyance of any kind. However, the papers will probably be bought by, or for, Yale. The University of Texas made overtures, but Pound's daughter, Mary, favored Yale. The major roadblock to any transfer seems to be the fact that Mrs. Ezra Pound still functions as the Committee for Ezra Pound, and would seem to legally control the papers. However, she is (or was, when I last heard from her) in the process of setting up some sort of trust. As a matter of interest, the Academic Center and Undergraduate Library of the University of Texas held a symposium on March 15-17, 1967, "Make it New: Translations and Metrical Innovation; Aspects of Ezra Pound's Work." Many first editions of Pound's writings were on display.

Part Four

1. At the first Washington hearing one of the psychiatrists referred to Pound as a Fascist. The poet jumped to his feet and shouted, "I never did believe in Fascism, God damn it! I am opposed to Fascism."

2. *Thrones, 96-109 de los Cantares.* New Directions, New York, 1959.

3. Giovannini attached these comments to a copy of Pound's letter to Secretary of State Herter. He is not certain at this point, almost ten years later, that this is an exact translation of the letter to *Illustrazione Italiana,* although he thinks it is at least a paraphrase. In any case, it represents Pound's views on the issuance of money and brings the letter to Secretary Herter into focus.

4. Prince Boris de Rachewiltz. Pound refers here to his distinguished career as an Egyptologist. *Love Poems of Ancient Egypt,* translated by Pound and Noel Stock (New Directions, Norfolk, Connecticut, 1962), are based on literal renderings of the hieroglyphic texts into Italian by Boris, which first appeared in the volume *Liriche Amorose degli Antichi Egizioni* (Vanni Scheiwiller, Milan, 1957).

5. Allen Upward (1863-1926), native of Worcester, educated at the Royal University of Ireland. Author of numerous romances; a play, *A Flash in the Pan;* and a number of works of non-fiction, including *A Day's Tragedy, Treason,* and *Some Personalities.* Basil Bunting, English poet, has been neglected, as Pound points out, but he seems to be coming into his own at last. *Poetry* recently devoted almost an entire issue to his poems, and the Academy of American Poets sponsored a New York reading early in 1967. His last two collections, *Loquitur,* Fulcrum Press, London, 1965, and *Briggflatts,* published by the same company in 1966, have been well received. Dorothy Pound sent these volumes to me from London, with a note: "A good *disciple* of EP's—but not an imitator." Pound dedicated *Guide to Kulchur* to Louis Zukofsky and Basil Bunting, "strugglers in the desert."

6. Eva Hesse.

7. "Miss Bleach" is Sylvia Beach, who opened a bookshop in Paris in 1919, named it Shakespeare and Company, and published James Joyce's *Ulysses* in book form.

8. In the spring of 1959 the United States Information Service arranged an exhibit of the works of American writers who lived in France during the 1920's. Some of Pound's books were included in the display, which was held in Paris.

9. When poetry by his friends was turned down, the poet took this as a personal affront. This may have happened in the case of *Poetry,* and prompted his statement. I do not know that Pound sent anything to *Poetry* while Karl Shapiro was editor, but some of his poems were published in the Golden Anniversary issue, and the editor, Henry Rago wrote me, "I was proud and happy to have that manuscript." The citation accompanying the award of the $500 Harriet Monroe award follows:

A Special Citation

"The generous person who for twenty-six years has been the anonymous donor of the Harriet Monroe Memorial Prize has made the prize this year five hundred dollars, instead of the usual one hundred, in observance of Poetry's fiftieth anniversary, and has suggested to the editor that he might open this award to all poets who have contributed to *Poetry* in any year since its beginnings in 1912. He gladly takes this option and, in consultation with the other judges, finds the task of choosing one poet from so vast and distinguished a field a surprisingly easy one. There is one inevitable choice: the great poet who from his first appearance in the first number has contributed to this magazine. . . ." A long list of poems follows. The citation continues:

EZRA POUND

"That the prize bears the name of the founder of *Poetry* makes this choice all the more pleasing. No other person in the history of this magazine helped her as much to do the proudest things that *Poetry* has done. And it is not displeasing to notice that for herself, Mr. Pound has recorded in the Harriet Monroe Memorial issue of *Poetry*, December 1936, what that collaboration, in the final balance, seemed to him." Pound's generous tribute to Miss Monroe follows, then the citation continues: "This prize is meant to honor a poet, and in doing so to honor a memory. The editor only wishes that all choices could be made with such transparent justice, and with the effect of so precise a testimony."

10. William Carlos Williams, *A Voyage to Pagany*. MaCauley Company, New York, 1928.

11. Pound's Four Point Program is spelled out in his *Introductory Text Book* published at Rapallo, Italy in 1938. Each of the four chapters is an elaboration of the following four quotations:

Chapter I

"All the perplexities, confusion, and distress in America arise, not from defects in their constitution or nonfederation, not from want of honour and virtue, so much as from downright ignorance of the nature of coin, credit, and circulation."

John Adams.

Chapter II

". . . and if the national bills issued, be bottomed (as is indispensable) on pledges of specific taxes, for their redemption within certain and moderate epochs, and be of proper *denomination for circulation*, no interest on them would be necessary or just because they would answer to everyone of the purposes of the metallic money withdrawn and replaced by them."

Thomas Jefferson (1816 letter to Crawford)

Chapter III

". . . and gave to the people of this Republic THE GREATEST BLESSING THEY EVER HAD—THEIR OWN PAPER TO PAY THEIR OWN DEBTS."

Abraham Lincoln

Chapter IV

The Congress shall have power:
To coin money, regulate the value thereof and of foreign coin and to fix the standards of weights and measures.

Constitution of the United States, Article 1, Legislative Department, Section 8, p. 5.

Done in the convention by the unanimous consent of the States, 7th September, 1787, and of the Independence of the United States the twelfth. In witness whereof we have hereunto subscribed our names.

George Washington
President and Deputy from Virginia.

12. D. G. Bridson, of the British Broadcasting Corporation's Third Pro-

gramme Staff, was one of the producers of the TV series on Churchill and also recorded a number of American poets for B.B.C. presentation. His radio play, *The Quest of Gilgamesh*, won the Italia Prize in 1956.

13. Noel Stock, *Poet in Exile*. Barnes and Noble, New York, 1964.

14. *Sewanee Review*. Sewanee, Tennessee (winter, 1966).

15. *Ezra Pound, Perspectives*, edited by Noel Stock. Henry Regnery Company, Chicago, 1965.

Index

213